A
PROCESSION
OF
Angels

A PROCESSION OF *Angels*

TRUE STORIES OF GOD'S MESSENGERS

EDITED BY EVELYN BENCE

Foreword by Colleen Hughes, Editor-in-Chief of *Angels on Earth*

Guideposts
New York, New York

A Procession of Angels

Published by Guideposts
16 East 34th Street
New York, New York 10016
www.guideposts.com

Acknowledgments

Every attempt has been made to credit the sources of copyrighted material used in this book. If any such acknowledgment has been inadvertently omitted or miscredited, receipt of such information would be appreciated.

Scripture quotations marked (KJV) are taken from *The King James Version of the Bible.*

Scripture quotations marked (NIV) are taken from *The Holy Bible, New International Version.* Copyright © 1973, 1978, 1984 International Bible Society. Used by permission of Zondervan Bible Publishers.

Scripture quotations marked (NKJV) are taken from *The Holy Bible, New King James Version.* Copyright © 1997, 1990, 1985, 1983 by Thomas Nelson, Inc.

Scripture quotations marked (RSV) the *Revised Standard Version of the Bible.* Copyright © 1946, 1952, 1971 by Division of Christian Education of the National Council of Churches of Christ in the U.S.A. Used by permission.

Cover design by Marisa Jackson
Cover image by Corbis
Interior design by Gretchen Schuler-Dandridge
Typeset by Aptara

Printed and bound in the United States of America
10 9 8 7 6 5 4 3 2 1

Contents

Foreword

This compilation, *A Procession of Angels*, holds some of the best angel stories I've ever seen. And I've read many wonderful life-changing stories in my years as editor-in-chief of *Angels on Earth*, the only magazine in the world devoted to angels and the role they play in our lives.

The stories here are unique; they prove how devoted the angels are to us, how they come in and out of our lives every day to comfort, to protect, to guide. You'll see that angels truly are everywhere, and while the fact of their presence may be surprising, they often appear in the most common places: in a flower shop and a high school auditorium, on a mountain trail and a sandy beach. Angels surround a sick baby's crib; they hold back the flames of a house fire. But angels also come to us in the most unlikely situations. An angel helps a rancher round up his cattle, sidles up to a runner in a marathon. One angel is heard over a CB radio; another offers free tickets to a sold-out baseball game. Angel encounters can happen at home in this country—on North Carolina's Outer Banks or at Kennedy Space Center—and as far away as Rome, the Philippines or Sudan. The angels know no boundaries. They travel on the winds of grace.

A Procession of Angels tells the story of the heavenly beings who are with us on our daily journey, ducking in and out of our lives, leaving traces of their presence and evidence of their love. They are truly messengers from God who reassure us that we never walk alone.

Colleen Hughes
Editor-in-Chief, *Angels on Earth*

Introduction

I grew up in a church that didn't emphasize ceremony or liturgy. As the organ played at the beginning of a worship service, the pastor and choir walked in from a side room. Taking their seats on the platform, they waited for the prelude to finish. The service really began when the first congregational hymn was announced. Then we all joined in, singing praises. The church I attend now is more formal and liturgical. Worship starts with instrumental music and more—a procession that symbolically brings God's gifts to the congregation and the congregation's gifts to God.

As I reflected on the movement implied by our title *A Procession of Angels,* my thoughts turned to this majestic church-aisle procession. I mentally changed the scene and imagined watching a host of parading angels, band after band descending from heaven to earth, each having a separate role to fulfill, a different type of ministry to perform. Traditionally angels have been categorized into nine orders: seraphim, cherubim, thrones, dominions, virtues, powers, principalities, archangels and angels. But our stories in this volume lend themselves to more sensual or material groupings. I started to ask questions:

What would a procession of angels look like? What angelic quality would lead the holy parade?

At church, on holy days and special celebrations, the church procession is led by an incense bearer, who wafts fragrance that represents prayers. We're like the psalmist who prayed, Lord, "let my prayer be set before thee as incense" (Psalm 141:2 KJV). In the angelic realm, anecdotal evidence indicates that visitations are sometimes accompanied by a sweet aroma, as if the grace of God floated in the breeze like a floral perfume. So that's where our line-up begins, with several authors telling their intriguing stories of angels radiating fragrance.

In a procession, incense is followed by a cross and candles, the light of Christ shining forth into the world. The chapter featuring a band of angels "shining with heavenly light" opens with a dramatic war story that climaxes with the sky itself sending an unforgettable visual message to soldier David Bell.

Although music precedes and accompanies the whole procession, a choir typically follows the cross and candles. Just as the choir's joyful singing adds another element of the spiritual sensual experience, so our heavenly procession continues with stories of angels who strengthen, comfort and inspire mortals with their otherworldly music.

A church procession winds down with marching ministers—lay and ordained—who are appointed to read the Word and deliver the gifts of God to the people of God. In parallel fashion, here the framework of our book opens to include true stories of God's messengers carrying out their ministries. You'll meet bands of angels delivering mercy, bringing hope, bolstering courage, speaking prophetically, ensuring livelihoods, dramatically altering life paths. One section features special stories about God's care of children, some written by loving parents, some written as childhood memories retained and cherished over a lifetime.

Finally, we turn to stories that portray angels as heavenly escorts at the end of this mortal life—coming to carry us home to a world beyond this island earth.

Turn the page. Start reading the story of Michelle Carpenter's miraculous healing, and you'll soon find yourself pleasantly "lost" in the midst of a procession of angels, sent by God to assure his people with signs of his love.

Evelyn Bence

A
PROCESSION
OF
Angels

1

DIFFUSING FRAGRANCE

In her story "A Huge Bouquet of Flowers," Pam Kidd notes, "When angels visit the earth, they sometimes announce their presence with the scent of flowers, especially roses." And that's where we'll start our procession of heavenly messengers. The first band of angels makes its presence known with a sweet aroma. To four people in need of comfort and strength, God's messengers bring healing and peace and a memory that inspires their faith.

Even if you've never had a similar aromatic awareness of God's care and keeping, I trust you can personalize this centuries-old prayer by John Tauler: "May Jesus Christ, the king of glory, help us to make the right use of all the myrrh that God sends, and to offer to him the true incense of our hearts."

Scent of a Rose

MICHELLE CARPENTER

*E*verything in my life was falling into place. I'd found David, the man of my dreams. We had just gotten married and moved to Hays, Kansas, where David was president of Hadley Regional Medical Center. One Friday afternoon I went to the medical center for an appointment. David promised me a romantic lunch when I was done. It was just a follow-up to my annual physical. My regular doctor had noticed symptoms that might indicate multiple sclerosis, and he recommended an MRI to rule it out.

After the MRI, David and another doctor were waiting for me. *Something's wrong*, I thought. "What's the matter?" I said. "Do you have to cancel our lunch?"

David shook his head and sat me down in the chair next to him. "This is our chief radiologist." David took both my hands in his. "Michelle, they found a tumor in your brain." His voice broke. "They think it's cancer."

The doctor described my condition and treatment. He pointed to a white, egg-sized mass above my right ear on my MRI. The recommendation was to see Dr. Orrison, a top neuroradiologist in Albuquerque, for surgery. We had to act fast. Numb and confused, David and I rushed home, packed our bags, and headed to New Mexico.

Several days later, I was lying on a hospital gurney in Albuquerque, head shaved. Was my life over? I was thirty years old. Death—my death—hadn't given me a worry. I remembered the first time I had thought about dying. It was the day of my baptism. I was ten. I lay back on my father's arms, and he slowly dunked my body in the warm water. Seconds later, he pulled me up and helped me to my feet. I hugged Dad as he dried me off, rubbing my long blonde hair with a towel. "God has a place for you in heaven," Dad said. "A special place just for you." He made the end of this life sound so peaceful. Then Dad reached around his back and handed me a rose. It was the first flower anyone had ever given me. I buried my nose in its soft velvety petals. I carry the scent of that rose with me in my memory to this day.

I turned my head. David was standing in the doorway, talking to Dr. Orrison. I felt a knot in my stomach. *Lord, if it's my time, I know that it's your will. Please be with David. Give him strength.* Quickly I tried to compose myself as David walked back into the room.

"How's my girl?" He kissed me.

"Well, no more bad hair days," I said. "You loved my hair. I must look awful."

"I love you, not your hair—and you're just as beautiful as ever."

I grabbed his hand. "Seriously, David," I said, "I need to know that you're going to be okay if I don't pull through. You've got a lifetime ahead."

"I won't give up on us." David paused for a moment and laughed. "We've only been married a year! Mrs. Carpenter, you're still under warranty." He gave me another kiss before the orderlies wheeled me into the operating room.

Waking up, I could only see blurry figures. My head was throbbing. "I'm cold," I whispered. A nurse wrapped blankets around me.

"Michelle?" a man's voice said from above. "Can you hear me?"

"Yes."

"Do you know what season it is?"

The question brought me out of my haze. David. I could see David. "It's the first day of dove-hunting season," I said, knowing how much he loved hunting.

"What?" Dr. Orrison said.

"I think she's okay," David said.

My prognosis wasn't good. The tumor was high-grade malignant and its roots had metastasized throughout my brain. I would undergo radiation treatments five days a week for the next two months.

I got used to the hospital routine. I went into a room and lay down on a cold table. A nurse lined the machine up to the dots tattooed on my scalp and walked out of the room. The machine sent high doses of radiation through my brain. One day, on the way home, I was feeling particularly weak and nauseous. David stopped at a red light and looked at me.

"When you're better, how about a second honeymoon?" he asked. "Hawaii?"

"Hawaii," I said. "I've always wanted to learn to surf."

"I was thinking more about a few moonlit walks on the beach," David said. We laughed as the light turned green. We needed the dream. But I knew I was living on borrowed time.

That night I lay in bed waiting for David. The bathroom door was ajar, and I watched him washing his face. *I may never see him do that again,* I thought. Every moment I had left with David was a gift. He shut off the bathroom light and got in bed. I slid close to him and brushed his hair off his forehead as he drifted off to sleep. I closed my eyes.

I turned over. *Must be the middle of the night.* I smelled something wonderful . . . the delicate, sweet scent of roses. The aroma was intoxicating and heady. Two chairs and a table appeared before me. I sat down. A single rose lay on the table. *I must be dreaming.*

"You're not dreaming, Michelle," a young woman said. She glided across the room toward me. Her hair was brown, wavy and parted down the middle. Her lips were full, her cheeks flushed and her eyes the color of honey. An ethereal light glowed from within her.

"Don't be afraid," she said. "My name is Rose. I'm here to help." She sat down.

"Am I dying?" I said. "I'm not afraid, but I am worried about my husband."

"You'll have more time with him," she said. "One day I'll show you the way to heaven. On that day, God will heal the hearts of those you leave behind. Now you have more to do, more life to live, more people to touch."

She hugged me, and I smelled the fragrance of roses lingering on her skin. In her arms, I felt strong and healthy. Rose pulled back from the hug. She put a hand on my head. A vibration ran through me. She stepped back and was gone. Light streamed through our window. I woke David. "Something incredible just happened," I told him.

That was fourteen years ago. Now every time I've seen Dr. Orrison, the MRI has been free of cancerous cells.

I've become a hospice volunteer. I try to ease the fears of those going to heaven and hold the hands of those left behind. Sometimes, when the moment is right, I tell them about Rose.

A Huge Bouquet of Flowers

PAM KIDD

On Holy Thursday 1984 I volunteered a few hours in my daughter's second-grade classroom and then brought her home. Keri and I were both anticipating the holiday weekend: On Good Friday, my mother and father were driving from Chattanooga to Nashville to visit us.

But when I pulled in the driveway, my husband David stood waiting for me on the front stoop. "Pam, I'm sorry," he said. "Your father has had a heart attack."

"Then we need to go right away to be there."

"Pam, he's dead."

How did I respond to those words? I consciously inhaled—and wondered if I would be able to exhale. If Daddy had lost his breath, would I lose mine? I was actually surprised that the air emptied from my lungs. One breath, then two. I was alive!

While David got the family ready to travel, I walked out to the spring that flowed through the back of the property. *This is when I'm going to break down, lose control, maybe even my breath,* I thought. But in the sound of the flowing water, I found a peace beyond my mortal understanding. I was breathing on my own. Alive! I had wonderful memories.

I had no regrets. As for Daddy, he'd gone quickly, as he'd always hoped. He was with his Lord and smiling down on me with the love that would never leave his face.

Early evening we drove into my parents' driveway in Chattanooga. The cross-shaped dogwood blossoms hung like an umbrella over my father's manicured grass, blooming tulips and trimmed rosebushes. Yet the red brick colonial house had a barren look. Daddy himself wasn't standing on the stoop, waving his hearty welcome.

Both of my children, Brock and Keri, bounded out of the car. After hugs and hellos from their grandmother, whom we all called Bebe, they headed straight for Pa's workshop. I sensed a child's wild hopes that maybe, just maybe, they'd find him there. He'd be waiting for them. He'd be laughing that the story of his death had been a joke.

David and I joined my mother in the den, eager to rehash the details of the day. Away on an overnight business trip to Birmingham, Daddy had died alone in a hotel room while getting dressed for breakfast. His body would be sent back to Chattanooga, to arrive before morning.

Suddenly my mother grew agitated and yet very focused. "Are the kids in the shop?" she asked.

"Yes, Bebe," I answered, "they needed to see his room."

"Oh, David. Go there right now. There's a loaded gun on the second shelf, on the left. Ever since that robbery, Harrison has left it . . . Hurry. If Brock picks it up—" A month before, a thief had plundered their house, even their bedroom, while they slept. They'd installed a security system, but Daddy had apparently still been nervous.

David ran out of the room, my mother and I following behind. "I don't see it, Bebe," David said. "Pa must have put it away."

"No. It was right here," she said as she entered. She turned to the shelving on the left and placed her palm on the second shelf. "Right here."

Keri spoke up. "Here's what *I* found on that shelf. An Annie doll. Pa left it for me."

"But did you see a gun?" Bebe asked.

"No." Neither Keri nor Brock had seen a weapon, though they had obviously canvassed the room. The shelf was well above the children's heads, but they had climbed on the footstool looking for treasure. On that same shelf, Brock had found a pocket knife with his name—in Daddy's handwriting—on the box.

Before we left the room, we all searched, and we all agreed: no gun—toy or real, loaded or empty.

Even so, Bebe suggested the kids leave the shop. She shut the door behind us, and we returned to the den and the cares and carings that come with death. A neighbor stopped with a casserole. The phone rang. We made calls and plans. And finally, we went to sleep, exhausted.

While most people downsize when their children leave home, my parents had bought a larger house to make room for their grandchildren. The room I now considered "mine" had some of my childhood furnishings. But when I'd married, Bebe had replaced my twin beds with one black iron bed, big enough for two. And "my" first-floor bedroom had no windows. When you went to bed, closed the door and turned off the light, the room was positively black.

I slept soundly until, deep in the night, I woke with a start. *Someone* was in the room, standing near the foot of the bed. I heard nothing except David's sleepy breath, and yet I knew an intruder was there. *The thief. He's returned.* The thought had hardly lodged in my mind when the scent of flowers came to my nostrils. I smelled a spring bouquet heavy with the sweetness of roses. Slowly, I turned toward David in the pitch dark. He hadn't stirred. As I leaned back toward the presence, the aroma wafted stronger and sweeter than before.

I lay mystified, no longer fearful, yet still certain, absolutely certain, that someone was standing near the foot of my bed. And this someone was holding a huge bouquet of fragrant flowers. After what seemed five or ten minutes, the presence left, stealing the fragrance away.

Not wanting to wake David, who sleeps soundly and cannot go back to sleep if disturbed, I slipped out of bed and went upstairs to my mother's room.

"Bebe."

She answered immediately, as if she hadn't been sleeping.

"I woke up and knew there was someone in my room. A visitor . . ." When I'd finished my story, she slipped on her robe. We two cased the house, room by room, up and down, looking and sniffing like police dogs. We even opened the door and turned on the light in the furnace room. Nothing was out of place. What's more, nothing smelled remotely like flowers.

Had the someone been Daddy? The thought crossed my mind, but I wasn't convinced. "Bebe, in the summertime, remember, Daddy would get up early and cut a rose in the garden? He'd sneak in my room and put it in the vase on my bedside table. When I woke up it was there, still wet with the dew."

She smiled. He did love his flowers. Leaving on his Wednesday trip, his last words to her had been "I love you," as he handed her a big bunch of tulips.

Finally we detectives dropped our fruitless investigation and went back to bed, drawing no real conclusions except that everything seemed perfectly under control.

The next morning my brother arrived, and we went to the funeral home. The memory of the unseen presence and the gift of fragrance bolstered the peace I'd first felt sitting by the spring in my own backyard. . . .

A year later, we drove home to Bebe's when the springtime flowers were in luscious bloom. The dogwood crosses again formed a canopy over the backyard. As usual, we all went into Daddy's shop to reminisce awhile. In that room we most keenly felt his presence; it's where he'd left his clearest mark.

Bebe and I sat down in the hard-back chairs, and she brought up a subject she'd mentioned repeatedly in the past year: Daddy's gun. The loaded 9-mm pistol that she'd never unearthed, though she had torn the shop apart—in an old-fashioned, housecleaning manner—looking for it.

Bebe turned to David, leaning against the shelf where Keri had found her Annie doll the night Pa died. "You know, David, I never did find that gun," she said.

Without comprehending what he might be saying, David answered, "You mean this gun?"

Bebe nearly lost her senses. There inside its unzipped case lay Dad's pistol. A yellow note was stuck to the outside of the wrapper. In big black letters, unmistakenly Daddy's scrawl, the note said, "Do not touch. Loaded." And indeed it was.

"*Nobody* has been in this room," Bebe assured us—and herself. "We have the security system . . . I cleaned every inch of this room myself, including that shelf. You all were *here* when we looked for it last spring. Now it appears, exactly where Harrison left it. What's going on?"

Of course, this side of heaven I'll never *know* who brought me a floral bouquet the night of Daddy's death. And the gun? I kept wondering, *What was going on?* My husband did not sneak that gun onto the shelf. Bebe is a good housekeeper, and she did not dust around the weapon.

For two more years these mysteries puzzled me. Then, on a 1987 vacation in Mexico, I received a clue from an elderly tour guide showing us an ornate angel statue in a historic church in Mexico City. His lecture included information about the art but also about angels themselves. One line caught my attention: "When angels visit the earth, they sometimes announce their presence with the scent of flowers, especially roses."

When angels visit . . . especially roses! I couldn't get the thought out of my mind.

Back home, I read everything about angels I could get my hands on. If you go looking for angelic accounts, you do see a pattern; over and over I read descriptions of the sweet smell of flowers.

I choose to believe that God sent two angels the day Pa died. One to give blessing: flowers in the night to soothe my soul. And one to take away danger: the gun my father had left out, not knowing my children might go bounding into his shop in his absence.

In a difficult time of personal loss, the biblical Job had the grace to say, "The Lord gave and the Lord has taken away; may the name of the Lord be praised (Job 1:21 NIV).

When I think of my father—his breath and his death—I whisper Job's prayer of praise.

When I think of the angels guarding my family—well, sometimes David and the kids roll their eyes. They think I've become an angel fanatic. It's probably best that they don't know that when I'm going someplace alone, I clear the front passenger seat of the car—to remind myself that my angel is there.

My Sweet Aunt Rosa

COLLEEN MESSINA

Great-aunt Rosa's bedroom was her sanctuary. She loved to read her Bible surrounded by the wallpaper she'd picked out herself—big, lush pink and red cabbage roses, so real-looking you could almost smell the sweet flower she'd been named for. Toward the end of her life, Rosa was confined to the hospital. After she died my parents moved into her house.

I found myself thinking about Rosa's room one afternoon, and I dialed her number. "I wish Aunt Rosa could have spent her last days in the room she loved best," I said to Dad.

"You know, I sat in there for a long while that day," Dad told me. "The smell of roses was intense and unmistakable. We could not figure out where it came from. The only roses in Rosa's room were the ones on the wallpaper." And, of course, the memory of Rosa herself, one of God's special flowers.

Healing Touch

FLORA REIGADA

I was always so tired. My husband and children were used to seeing me that way, but I couldn't accept it. I'd glance at my reflection in the mirror and wonder who that sad woman was. For years I'd lived with an irregular heartbeat and circulatory problems caused by diabetes. Doctors had done what they could. In the morning I did my best to ignore my racing heart and the pain in my legs, but I was a wreck by the end of the day. Even my prayers were tired. I just sort of checked in with God every now and then—routine, like managing the house and meeting the deadline for my newspaper column. I hadn't grown up in a religious family, so I didn't really know how to pray. My late mother-in-law had a deep faith, and she often read me stories from the Bible. *Faith should be perfect like hers,* I thought, *not like mine.* Talking to God meant you believed he was listening, and I wasn't so sure of that. A couple of years ago I wondered if God had given up on me. No surprise if he had. I often felt like giving up too.

One night, the chores after supper seemed to take forever. My heart was pounding, and I was almost too exhausted to stand. When my husband, Daniel, put the last plate in the dishwasher and switched it on, I breathed a sigh of relief. "I need to sit down and rest for a while, okay?" I said.

"Sure, Mom," said my son David. "Dad and I want to watch the game anyway." They headed for the living room, and I collapsed on the couch in the family room. I was glad to be left alone. My family was very supportive emotionally, helping me in every way possible, but as far as my physical comfort went, there was nothing anyone could do.

I kicked off my shoes. I reached down and lifted one leg and then the other, slowly stretching them out on the coffee table in front of me. My feet were cold and numb, and I winced at the sight of them—swollen and cracked, and an ugly shade of blue. I grabbed a blanket from the end of the couch and quickly covered myself. The blanket's warmth was comforting, and I snuggled into it.

Pain throbbed upward from my feet, and I pulled the blanket closer around my legs. That's what it came down to: We struggle alone in this world. I could imagine my mother-in-law disagreeing with me. Surely she would have known a Bible verse or story to prove that wasn't so. *God, forgive me,* I prayed. *My faith isn't perfect by a long shot.* And how could I expect God to help lessen my pain when my faith in him wasn't as strong as I knew it should be?

Leaning back, I closed my eyes and drifted off into sleep. The house was quiet when I woke up. I felt at peace, with none of the pain I'd had all day. *I must have died and gone to heaven,* I thought. Glancing down at my legs, I saw my feet were no longer on the table, but on the floor, sticking out from under the blanket. What I saw next seemed like the most beautiful of dreams, but my eyes were open. A young woman knelt in front of me, massaging my feet. She wore a long, flowing dress, and beneath soft brown hair her face shone with innocence. I knew without a doubt: I was looking at an angel. She was the only one I saw, but I felt the presence of others in the room like warming sunshine.

I sat up straight. *This can't be!* In that moment, my moment of doubt, the angel vanished. Sinking back into the couch, I shut my eyes, trying to recapture the image of that innocent, shining face again in my mind. I could still feel her comforting hands massaging my feet and the warmth of her presence. My pain was gone. *I haven't gone to heaven,* I thought. *Heaven has come to me.*

"Mom, you're smiling," David said the next morning. I wasn't aware of it. I glanced in the mirror, and it was true. I didn't see the sad woman anymore. "I'm feeling better," I said. Deep within, my heart still raced, and my swollen feet and legs tingled with pain. But I did feel better, even if only a little. I wanted to share my experience with my family, but I decided to keep the vision in my mind for a while. It seemed private, something I could hardly understand myself. And something I hardly deserved.

Not long after, I had another especially difficult day. Once again, when supper was over, I sought solace alone on the family room couch. Surfing through channels, my mind wandered, and I finally clicked off the TV. I wrapped the blanket around me and fell asleep. When my eyes opened, I looked down at my hands folded in my lap. Then I saw other hands emerging from translucent sleeves. They held a clear pitcher filled with golden oil, its fragrance drifting upward into the room. The oil was slowly poured over my hands, warming them, sending a soothing sensation through my whole body. *Like the Bible stories my mother-in-law read,* I realized. Perfumed oils used for healing.

I moved my hands, wanting to touch my healing messenger. Can this be real? Once again, my second of doubt caused the vision to disappear, and I was left alone. But at the same time, I knew I was anything but alone.

A third encounter occurred only days later, when I awoke on the couch to see a young woman at my side. She leaned close, seeming to whisper in my ear, but I heard no words. Instead, waves of peace coursed through me. For a few seconds I felt as if I had never known pain at all. *How can this be happening?* With one questioning thought, the woman was gone from my side.

In the days that followed, I carried these visions with me like my comforting blanket from the couch. My family got used to seeing me smile again. Eventually I shared my experiences with them and searched the Bible for stories about angels. I feel like those worshipers of old who peered through the portals of temples and churches for a glimpse of the Holy of Holies. Just like my health, my faith will never be perfect. But that didn't keep God from me. In his grace, he showed me three times that angels are ever near and devoted to my care, spiritually and physically.

2

SHINING WITH
HEAVENLY LIGHT

*Of his love, God has opened an occasional door, and has
assailed my eyes with as much light as they can now bear.*
—CHAD WALSH, *Behold the Glory*

After incense is diffused in the air, a church procession continues with a cross flanked by candles: the light of Christ shining in the world. So we next present stories of angels who are bathed in "the light of God's love," to use a phrase of Bobbie Ward in "Vigil for Lainey."

A wartime drama, "Close Enough to Touch" by David Bell, sets the stage for this section of stories in which angels guide the lost, bring healing to the distressed and soothe the suffering.

As you read these stories you may find encouragement for your own life, as you "walk as children of light . . . and try to learn what is pleasing to the Lord" (Ephesians 5:8, 10 RSV).

Close Enough to Touch

DAVID J. BELL

Today's soldiers are fighting wars in lands far from home, far from their loved ones, far from everything they know. I understand their loneliness and the fear in their hearts, because I felt it myself, nearly sixty-five years ago.

Forty-eight short hours after our wedding, I had to say good-bye to my bride. Marguerite and I weren't sure if or when we would see each other again. How could we have imagined when I bought her engagement ring on December 6, 1941, that our world would change the very next day? The Japanese attacked Pearl Harbor, and the United States entered World War II. I volunteered for the US Army. I was twenty years old, and I'd never ventured far from my small Tennessee town. But in a few months I found myself on a boat headed for the South Pacific as part of the First Signal Troop of the First Cavalry Division.

"I never dreamed I'd see the Pacific Ocean," I said to a buddy, "let alone cross it." But the war wasn't a dream. I shut my eyes in prayer. Like everyone on that ship, I was afraid.

We were bound for the Philippines, scene of some of the deadliest battles of the war and central to Japan's goal of controlling that vast area of the Pacific. Many island countries had been captured, but US-Filipino units maintained a resistance in the Philippines. We sailed on a zigzag path for three weeks because of the threat of enemy submarines. First Australia, then New Guinea and the Admiralty Islands. Places on a map, each one strange to us and farther from home. Letters were a lifeline, a sign that we soldiers weren't forgotten. In every port I hoped to hear "Bell!"—my name shouted out at mail call. It didn't always happen. Marguerite wrote me every day, but her letters sometimes took a month to arrive.

We landed in the Philippines in October 1944. There, for the first time, we were on the ground in a combat zone. We dug in. Jumping into foxholes during rocket attacks became a way of life. One night I scribbled a letter to Marguerite: "Today a plane zoomed over us so low I could see the insignia." *Can anyone back home understand?* I wondered. I was proud to serve my country, but I'd never known such fear and loneliness and distance from everything that was familiar. "Deliver us," the Lord's Prayer said. Was it possible? And if so, how long would it be before I returned home to Marguerite? We were told in the beginning that after eighteen months we would be rotated back to the States. But rotation was now out of the question. The Japanese had a stronghold on so many different islands in the South Pacific.

One evening the news came down that our division was scheduled to be among the first to invade Japan. "Well, that's it, I guess," a buddy said to me. We knew it would be a long battle with many casualties. *It might be years before I go home. If I'm lucky enough to be alive.* My hope was fading fast.

I didn't know how to go on, so I headed for the prayer services down by the river, led by a soldier whose ministerial training had been interrupted by the war. I looked around at the many soldiers in attendance that night. No matter. *This is a godforsaken place,* I thought.

A bright moon bathed us in light as we stood with bowed heads. The young soldier-minister talked to us in a reassuring tone. "God will not forsake us," he said. "God knows our every fear and longing. He sees our every move."

"Look!" someone said.

Men pointed to the sky. I glanced up. I was astounded by what I saw. Hovering directly above us was the shape of a cross. Because of the moon behind it, the clouds shone as if under a spotlight. I reached out my hand, love suddenly pounding in my heart like a drum. The cross seemed close enough to touch.

None of us moved as we gazed upward. Not a word was spoken. The lighted cross hovered above us for several minutes before the clouds drifted away. There we were, fighting a war thousands of miles from home, feeling as if we might never see our loved ones again, and then this. A sign from God like nothing anyone could have expected. I'd been wrong. We were not forsaken. However long it took to end the war, no matter what I faced along the way, God would be with me.

All these years later, I can still see that cross clearly in my mind's eye. Through the many seasons of my life, I have felt God's love as I did that night in the Philippines. Pounding in my heart. Close enough to touch. I wanted today's soldiers to know that, no matter what, they will not be forsaken.

A Familiar Light

ROBIN LANGSTON BEIERMEISTER

I tossed several shopping bags full of Christmas gifts into the backseat of my car and joined the stream of traffic fighting to get out of the mall parking lot. I was running late for my annual appointment with my gynecologist, which I had already put off for some time. Even without the seasonal hustle-bustle, I was busy looking after four daughters with my husband, Geoffrey. Besides, it didn't seem too pressing; I was thirty-seven and in good health. At the doctor's office I waited impatiently for the exam to be over with so I could go home and read Christmas stories to my "babies," two-year-old Hayley and four-year-old Ryan.

A few days later I got a phone call. The doctor said my Pap smear result was slightly abnormal and I should be tested again in a few months. *Just some mistake at the lab,* I thought. I felt fine and was so busy planning our holiday activities I didn't have time to worry. But three months later, when the second test also came back abnormal, my doctor scheduled a biopsy.

The day before the procedure I took a long walk, trying to calm my fears. As I turned a corner I came to a little gift shop. My eye was drawn to a beautiful gold cross in the window, gleaming in the rays of the late afternoon sun. I felt compelled to go in and buy it. Outside again, I clasped it around my neck and felt less afraid.

When the biopsy results were ready, a nurse called to set up an immediate appointment to come in and talk to the doctor. "Try not to worry," she said, but worry was all I could do. The next day, as I sat in the doctor's quiet office waiting for him to explain the test results, I kept reaching for the gold cross around my neck. He said the biopsy revealed well-defined cancer cells. I gripped the edge of his huge oak desk with both hands and closed my eyes. For the past seven months it had been just a nagging question mark on my medical chart. Now I had to accept the fact that I had a potentially deadly disease.

"We could schedule a full hysterectomy right now. Or we could do another procedure to find out more about what we're facing," the doctor said.

I shook my head and met his gaze. I didn't want to deal with uncertainty anymore. I just wanted things to get back to the way they were.

"No, I want the operation," I said.

He nodded. "It will be impossible to tell until the surgery how far-reaching the cancer is. But we'll have a specialist standing by in case it's spread beyond the cervix."

I went through the rest of the day with worries and regrets turning in my mind. Why had I put off the Pap smear for so long? What if the cancer had already spread?

That night I sat wearily on the edge of Ryan's bed as she finished saying her prayers.

"And please, God, take away the bad stuff that's making Mommy sick, so she can be happy again."

I pulled her close, my throat tightening, and then tucked her in quickly. I could not break down in front of my children. *Lord, give me the strength to endure this struggle.*

The night before my surgery I checked into the hospital for pre-op procedures. I wasn't allowed to eat anything. I had a bit of a sore throat, so I was given antibiotics through an IV line. I lay staring at the ceiling, just wanting the cancer out of me. I felt as though there were a huge clock ticking above my head, counting down the minutes till the disease would take over my whole body. I was racing against that clock.

By morning my sore throat had become a full-fledged fever. My doctor couldn't operate. He sent me home and rescheduled the surgery for ten days later. The fever persisted. When the new date arrived, my temperature was 104 degrees.

"Why is this happening? Can't you give me something?" I pleaded with my doctor on the phone.

"Robin, the tests show what you have isn't bacterial, so antibiotics aren't effective. The only thing I can tell you to do right now is wait the virus out. Stress and worry will only make it worse. Try to rest."

Easier said than done. Unable to look after my youngest children, I felt totally helpless. Geoffrey and my older girls took over their care and made sure there were always fluids and Tylenol by my bedside. My arms ached to hold my little ones, but I was so sick and weak I could hardly lift a water glass.

That night I lay in bed alone; Geoffrey had been sleeping downstairs because of my fever. I tossed and turned. How could I fight the cancer when this fever was making surgery impossible? What if it was already too late? Would my girls have to grow up without me?

I wrapped myself in the large violet-and-yellow quilt on the bed, my grandmother's favorite. I felt a sharp tug and looked down. My cross was caught in the threads of the quilt. I disentangled it and ran a finger over its surface. Then, squeezing it tightly in my palm, I began to pray. *God, please take away this fever so I can have the operation.* I had always had faith, but I had never prayed like that. Over and over, waking myself out of a fitful slumber, I begged God to make me well enough to have the surgery. I prayed without pride and without doubt. It felt as though I had reached the very core of my soul and my prayer was coming from there. Even as I continued to shiver and then sweat in the throes of fever, I asked him to send me help.

In the early hours of morning I awoke after a short doze. But I couldn't open my eyes and my body felt strange, as if it were gently vibrating. When I finally managed to raise my eyelids, I looked down and saw my body through the patchwork quilt bathed in a golden-green light that outlined my shape. My eyes followed the light to its source. Three beings who appeared to be composed of pure light were at the foot of the bed. A dazzling brightness spread out behind them like wings, and the beams that encircled me seemed to emanate from their hands. Now I was fully awake, fully aware.

For a moment I was terrified. Then I understood clearly the message, "You are safe. You are loved. Go back to sleep." I obeyed. But soon the enormity of what I was experiencing crept back into my mind and my eyes sprang open. I had to see what they were doing.

My body was still enveloped in light. I didn't dare move. The angel on the right tilted her head toward the one in the center as if to communicate something. *I know these angels,* I thought suddenly. *They have been with me before. They are here to help me.* With that realization I closed my eyes and slept soundly.

As the first rays of dawn spilled through the blinds, I woke and managed to roll out of bed and walk to the bathroom. I felt drained but also, somehow, energized.

Geoffrey was fixing his tie when he saw me. He pressed his hand against my forehead. "Honey, you're not hot anymore," he said, surprised. "Still, I want you to get back in bed. I'll give you a call later."

He hurried off to work and I splashed some water on my face. That's when I remembered. *Angels were here last night!* Again, I had the distinct impression that the angels had been with me all my life, that they would always be with me.

A week later I had the surgery. Just as I was waking up in post-op I again saw angels, floating among the curtained cubicles, observing patients. They didn't come to me or even look my way, but I knew intuitively that was because my crisis had passed. Later, the doctor came to give me the good news.

"It looks like we caught the cancer just in time, Robin. I think you'll make a full recovery. You're very lucky."

Three cancer-free years later I know I've been more than lucky. I've been blessed. My recovery from cancer is only part of it, though. I carry with me now the conviction that God's light shines on us always and never more brightly than in our darkest hours.

Light in the Darkness

ANNETTE HEATHERINGTON

The view from atop Grouse Mountain in Vancouver, British Columbia, Canada—2,800 feet high—is stunning. Tourists flock to the spot, riding up on a cable car named the Skyride. My friends and I liked to make the trek on foot. It was called the Grouse Grind, or Mother Nature's StairMaster. Part of the trail is man-made stairs, but mostly it's steep grades that wind through the forest.

I pulled into the parking lot and checked the clock on the dashboard: 6:30 PM. A half-hour late, but it was still daylight. *I hope the gang waited for me,* I thought. *I should have called to let them know I'd be late.* I looked around the parking lot. I didn't see anyone I knew. *Oh well, I'll just catch up.* I grabbed my water bottle and threw on my windbreaker over my T-shirt and running pants. I locked the car and headed to the park gate.

I'd gotten used to going it alone since my husband and I had separated. The divorce was almost final and I'd become self-sufficient. I discovered I could still enjoy the things I had done with my husband without him. I traveled, went to restaurants and movies. I even started hiking. *I don't need to be part of a group to do the Grouse Grind. I can hack it just fine.*

The sun would be going down soon. I took the steps by twos, breathing more quickly. With my friends I laughed and chatted the whole way up the mountain. Hiking by myself, I noticed every step. I got to a bridge made from a log and knew I was a quarter of the way up the mountain. *Keep it up,* I told myself.

Clouds rolled in. A sudden downpour soaked me. I dashed off the trail and huddled under a big tree. The dense forest was darker than the trail. Was it just the storm or was it later than I thought? Once night fell I would not be able to find my way along the path. Even staying on the steep trail could be dangerous. A slip on the stairs could mean falling into a ravine, spraining an ankle or worse. I had to get off the mountain fast. *Where am I?* I brushed my wet hair out of my eyes and squinted at the city lights dim in the distance.

I tried not to think about the people who'd gotten lost on Grouse Mountain. Some of them had died. I hugged my wet clothes to my body, shivering. *Am I closer to the bottom or the top? I passed the log bridge already. That's only a quarter of the way up. Closer to the bottom. Good.* Down was where the car was, so down I went.

I left the shelter of the big tree and found the trail again. Carefully I began my descent. The trail had turned to mud. I took a few steps and fell. Pain shot through my leg. I tried to straighten it. It hurt, but I could still move it. I limped along until I spotted a trail marker I recognized. *I'm closer to the top.* I slumped to the ground.

How am I going to find my way down? God, I was wrong. I thought I could do this alone, but I can't. I need you. It had been a long time since I'd admitted needing anyone. I don't know how long I sat there, shaking with cold and fear, my tears mingling with the raindrops.

Sniffling, I closed my eyes and breathed deeply. *Well, I'm not going to get off Grouse Mountain sitting here crying.* I calmed myself down a little. *You are independent,* I told myself, *but not alone. Never alone. God is here.*

I opened my eyes, determination renewed. I saw a beam of light. *Someone's found me!* "Help! I'm over here!" I cried. No response. It wasn't a flashlight beam. But what was it? Where was it coming from?

My leg was stiff, so I stayed on my knees. I crawled to the light. It moved ahead. *What is that?* I moved; the light moved. I looked behind me. Darkness. The light stayed a few feet in front of me, winding with the path. I followed.

I reached the log bridge again. *The quarter mark!* Encouraged, I struggled on, though my knees hurt and my hands stung from crawling on the rough terrain.

Finally, I made it to the bottom. *Time to try the leg again.* I crawled over to a tree. I grabbed hold of the trunk and pulled myself up. The light grew faint and disappeared. I staggered out of the woods. "Thank you," I said out loud.

My car was the only one in the parking lot. I fished the keys out of my pocket. My hands were shaking. Not with fear. This time with awe. Something amazing had happened on that mountain.

I couldn't wait to tell my friends about it. The question they all asked was, "Why were you hiking alone?" Now I know better. Just like I know to look for the light that guided me—out of darkness on Grouse Mountain and every day since.

Light over My Shoulder

ROBERT KIMBLE

I took real pride in graduating from Sultana High School. There, as one of 1,600 students, I had to look out for myself. I had to be responsible, to ask for help when I needed it. But long before, when I was just a kid, my sixth-grade teacher at a small private school had taught me how to do that.

Miss Basham encouraged all her students to go to her with our problems. She said her prayers might help. Go to a teacher? Willingly? The idea was new to me. But each morning before the bell rang, a couple of my classmates went up to her desk. I watched them sit next to Miss Basham, their eyes closed while she spoke softly. After a few minutes the kids went away looking peaceful. I started to think I was missing out on something. With both my parents working so much and my spending a lot of time home alone, I figured maybe I could use some extra prayer too. Eventually I took her up on her offer.

I sat down in a chair beside hers, and she listened closely as I told her about letting myself in the house after school, making my own dinner and sometimes even going to bed before my mother and father came home.

"Okay, Robert," she said when I finished, and asked me to close my eyes. "Dear Lord, Robert needs you," she whispered. "His parents work long hours and sometimes he gets lonely. Stay by his side, day and night."

I did feel good when I went back to my desk, as if the words she'd uttered in my name had gone straight to heaven. But there was something I kept to myself, something I was too embarrassed to tell her. It was more than being lonely. My neighborhood wasn't the safest, and sometimes I was afraid.

One Friday morning about halfway through the school year, I locked the front door behind me and headed to the bus stop. An unusually dense fog had settled over the streets and between the houses, and I walked fast. I never knew who might be lurking around, even at that early hour.

When I got to school Miss Basham greeted me at the door of our classroom. "Good morning, Robert," she said. "Would you like me to pray with you?" I was surprised. Miss Basham never asked a student if he wanted to pray. She waited for us to approach her, so we didn't feel pressured or uncomfortable. But with the weekend ahead and my parents at work for most of it, I said sure.

I followed her to her big wooden desk, and she pulled a chair up next to hers. Other kids were filing into the classroom, and I struggled to concentrate. I shut my eyes and repeated some of the words I'd heard Miss Basham use. "Stay by my side, Lord, day and night," I asked. I was thinking of tonight especially. Friday nights could be rowdy, with everybody partying and hanging out after the long week.

"God is watching over you, Robert," Miss Basham said, her voice slow and even. "He's got his strong hand on your shoulder. You are never alone."

Her words floated into the air around me and lingered there like that stubborn fog outside. I hoped they would do some good.

After school some of the guys and I shot hoops for a while. Then my friend Isaac invited me over to his house. We ate dinner with his family and watched some TV until we both got tired.

"Come on. I'll walk you part of the way," Isaac said, grabbing his jacket. It was pitch-black; the few streetlights had been shot out with BB guns—or worse.

Four blocks from my house, Isaac said good-bye and I picked up my pace. I hunched my shoulders and dug my fists deep into my pockets, picturing God's strong hand on my shoulder, like Miss Basham had said.

With my driveway in sight, I heard loud voices up ahead. Some older guys were talking and laughing while they spray-painted graffiti on a garage. I hoped I could pass by and get inside without their noticing. *Stay cool,* I told myself. *They won't mess with me if I mind my own business.*

Then I saw what they were painting: gang symbols. I recognized one of the guys. He had a bad rep and had been to jail. I slowed my gait and considered heading back to Isaac's, but it was too late.

The ex-con had seen me.

"That little punk's gonna call Five-0," he said, meaning the police. "Let's get him!" The pack surged toward me.

These guys were several years older than I was—and much bigger. I couldn't run home because they'd know where I lived. But I couldn't stay where I was either, not on my life. I didn't move. *Please, God, don't let them hurt me!* Eight guys formed a semicircle in front of me, blocking my path. One gave a sinister smile. Another made a move for his pocket. *Does he have a knife? Or a gun?*

The one I'd recognized seemed to be the leader. He reached out his hand as if he was going to grab me around the neck. Then all of a sudden he drew his arm back and covered his eyes. "Man," he said. "What is that?"

A bright light shone on the guys' faces. They all stepped back a few inches. The beam seemed to be coming from behind me, but I didn't dare take my eyes off the gang.

"Where'd he come from?" one guy muttered, staring up over my shoulder.

"I don't know, but how we gonna kill 'em both at once?" his friend answered.

Not one of the hoodlums was paying attention to me anymore; they were watching someone taller, someone standing behind me. I didn't care who it was. I was just grateful not to be alone.

Finally the leader glanced down at me again. "Aw, he's just a kid," he said, losing interest. A few others nodded in quick agreement. "Let's let him live." By now each of them, eyes still locked on someone behind me, was walking backward as quickly as he could. Then they all turned and took off running. Not one looked back.

When they were far gone, I looked over my shoulder. But the blinding spotlight had been turned off. There was no clue as to where it had come from.

Inside my house, I locked the door and hooked the safety chain. No one was home, but I didn't feel lonely. Or afraid. God had his strong hand on my shoulder, just as Miss Basham had said. That bright, protecting light? It had come straight down from heaven, in answer to my prayer.

Vigil for Lainey

BOBBIE S. WARD

*E*veryone said, "What a beautiful baby." I was her mom. Naturally I agreed. Named for my grandmother Sylvia and my mother, Elaine, little Lainey, as we called her, had shining blue eyes and porcelain skin. At four-and-a-half months, she was the picture of health.

But one night Lainey had difficulty breathing, and she pushed her bottle away. *Poor baby has a cold,* I thought. First thing the following morning, I took Lainey to her pediatrician. After an examination, the doctor sent us to Mercy Medical Center. "Something's wrong with her," I said when I called my husband, Dale, at work, "but they don't know what it is." Dale went home to take care of Timothy, our two-year-old, and I stayed with Lainey. A nurse came into the room and offered to get me something to eat or drink. I shook my head. All I could think of was my baby.

Lainey looked especially small in the oversized hospital gown. She breathed easier but not without a struggle. Her complexion was ashen. I held her tiny hand. "I promise never to leave you," I whispered. "Whenever you need me, I'm here." I trusted God to take care of her, but I wanted to help her too. It took all my will to keep from scooping her up in my arms.

About 11:00 PM another nurse came in. "I have something to help your daughter breathe," she said, putting a mask over Lainey's nose and mouth. When the nurse left the room I moved to sit on the other bed, across from Lainey. I ached to embrace my daughter but stopped myself. I worried I would disturb her. *Lord, I feel so helpless.*

I pulled the covers over me to sleep but checked on Lainey one more time.

The most extraordinary light surrounded her. I could make out four figures, defined within the light, humanlike but shaped out of the light itself. Two figures floated beneath Lainey's bed, as if supporting her. One floated at the head of the bed, the other at the foot. These two faced each other, covering my child with their luminous arms, embracing her with light. They seemed intent on their vigil.

I wondered if they were angels sent by God. I hadn't asked in words, but the figure at the head of the bed looked at me and nodded yes. Then, in the blink of an eye, the four angels vanished. I hadn't been to sleep at all, but I felt revitalized and reassured. In an instant, God gave me more strength than I had ever known before.

That strength was much needed. Lainey took a turn for the worse the next day. She was transported to Dayton Children's Medical Center.

"We're fairly certain she has viral pneumonia," Dale and I were told. Lainey had only a 50-percent chance of survival. I couldn't watch while the nurse put an IV into Lainey's hand. Instead, I pulled her room door open and hurried into the hallway. I leaned against the wall, listening to Lainey cry. Only twenty-four hours earlier my child had been healthy. Now she was in danger. What could I do? I went to the rest room to wash up, and a strange face looked at me from the mirror, streaked with black from mascara and tears. "Look what you've done to yourself," I said. I thought about the four angels. I reminded myself that God was in control. I knew whatever happened, I could rely on His power.

Further tests revealed birth defects in Lainey's heart. Left untreated, she'd die of congestive heart failure. She was transferred immediately to Cincinnati Children's

Hospital for open-heart surgery—a complex operation in the tiny heart of a four-month-old.

After a long procedure, Dale and I received the good news we'd prayed for: The surgery was a success. But one problem remained: Lainey's pulmonary pressure was too high. "There may be permanent lung damage," the doctor said. Our parents and other family members and friends had come to Cincinnati to be with us—twelve people in all. We were allowed to see Lainey two at a time. Each of us talked to Lainey, and we gently placed our hands on her head. "The worst part is over," I said to her. "God and his angels are with you." Soon after our prayers and the warm touch of our hands, Lainey's pulmonary pressure returned to normal. The vigil was over.

Today our daughter is once more the picture of health. Sometimes she'll ask me about what happened, and I tell her about the angels. "God is always with us," I say. "He sent messengers that night so we could see the light of his love." He showed me that Lainey was in his care, then and forever.

Light in the Mist

HELEN BLIDE

ain pattered down on the car as my daughter Lisa and I crossed the border from New York into Sussex County in New Jersey. We were on our way home from visiting my mother. A cardboard box slid back and forth on the backseat. Mom had insisted we take what looked like several meals' worth of her delicious home-cooked Polish food. "Share it with your friends," Mom had said. That was my immigrant mother. She never forgot the years our family had struggled when I was growing up and was always thinking of other families who might need help too.

"Hey," Lisa said, sitting up beside me. "Sussex County. Isn't this where Martha lives?"

"This is the place," I said sadly. My friend's warm, friendly face seemed to rise up before my eyes, as if she were right there with us. "But I don't know where exactly."

Losing Martha was one of the most painful things in my life. When she lived down the road, the two of us saw each other all the time. We worked out together to keep in shape, went antique shopping, talked about our children. Martha had two, a boy and a girl. When her marriage broke up, she and the children moved. I wouldn't let distance come between us; I wanted to give them all the support I could. Sometimes Martha felt like more than a friend—more like the sister I had never had.

The rain stopped, replaced by a swirling mist. I'd made this trip a hundred times. I knew where I was going. *Martha's somewhere out in that mist,* I thought as I turned on my high beams. *I just don't know where.*

On an ordinary afternoon about a year before, I'd dropped by the farm where Martha lived as a caretaker to say hi. The place was empty. A sign announced the farm had been sold. Martha was gone—no forwarding address, no good-bye. Nothing. Rumor around town said she'd moved to Sussex County, but I'd never been able to track her down.

I slowed the car as I approached a fork in the road. *God,* I asked, *watch over Martha. If she needs my help, let her get in touch!*

I prepared for a right turn and stopped. *What's that?* I thought, peering through the windshield. A bright beam of light cut through the mist in the distance. I had to follow it.

I took the left fork.

"Mom, where are we going?" Lisa asked. "This isn't the way home."

"I know," I said. "But I have the strangest feeling that Martha lives right around here somewhere."

The light led us down a dead-end road. We came out of the mist. In front of us stood an old white stucco farmhouse with a red barn.

"Do you think this is it?" asked Lisa.

"Yes," I said. "I do." But how could I possibly know that? I'd never seen this farm before in my life. All those trips to visit Mom, and I'd never once wondered what was down the other fork in the road. Could it really be Martha? "You stay in the car," I told Lisa. "I'll make sure we're at the right place."

I knocked. A little girl opened the door. Blonde pigtails coming loose, a smudged face and sad blue eyes. Her brother came up behind her. "Helen!" he said. "I'm glad you're here. I think Mom could use a friend right now."

I could see dirty dishes stacked in the sink. A pile of laundry in the corner. The house was cold. It smelled musty. *This isn't like Martha.*

"Mom's in the barn."

"Stay here with the kids," I told Lisa who had now come inside the house. I hurried to the barn, my boots sinking in the mud. Faster and faster, as if I might be too late. *Too late for what?*

I pushed open the door. *Martha!* She was standing on the upper level of the barn, looking down at the piles of hay below her. Martha's back was to me. Bits of straw stuck to her green sweater and uncombed hair.

"Martha?" I said. "Is everything okay?"

She looked down at me. Martha's face was pale as a ghost, and she had dark circles under her eyes. She gave a sigh full of sadness and exhaustion but didn't seem able to speak.

I hurried up to put my arms around her. "Talk to me," I said, stroking her hair. "We've been friends a long time."

It took her a moment to get the words out. "Things got real bad, you see," she said. "I lost my job. I ran out of money. I didn't know what to do or where to turn. Then tonight..." She forced herself to get the words out. "I was going to do something drastic."

"Oh, Martha!" I said, holding her tight. "I'm so glad you didn't."

"Something stopped me," Martha said. She looked at me with her eyes full of wonder. "I asked God to send me an angel. And then an image of your face appeared in my mind."

"I'm not an angel," I said. "But it was an angel who led me to this farmhouse tonight."

I walked Martha back to the house, where Lisa and I unpacked Mom's delicious food. Martha's family would have a good dinner tonight. Then we could start work on those dishes and the laundry.

Martha's life changed for the better soon afterward. She got a new job, a new house— she even fell in love. She moved again, all the way to Florida. But this time she left me an address and phone number, and promised she would call if she ever needed anything or just wanted to talk. I was ready to listen. What's more, so was God.

3

MAKING MUSIC

Music is well said to be the speech of angels.
—THOMAS CARLYLE

At Christmastime we sing of angel choirs, but there's nothing seasonable about the scope of the otherworldly music heard by writers in this section. Young Melanie Emory tells a particularly dramatic story of hearing heavenly praises that seemed to confirm that she was right where God wanted her to be—"In the Hollow of His Hand" and moving toward a future of promise. And Shony Alex Braun's story of survival in Dachau might well give you the shivers.

In response to stories of the music-making band of angels, I started to sing a song from Isaiah 12:2 that has been in my mind much of the day: "Surely it is God who saves me. I will trust in him and not be afraid" (*Book of Common Prayer*). By the time you've finished reading this section, I trust your heart will also be overflowing with praises.

Memory for the New Year

LOIS LONNQUIST

I stood at our picture window on a January night last year. A strong west wind was bending the branches of our birch tree, sending swirls of snow across the lawn. I touched my fingertips to the icy glass, closed the drapes and then sat down on the couch, wrapping myself in my new Christmas robe.

I had gone to bed earlier, but after tossing and turning for an hour I had finally given up and gone into the living room to think things out. That afternoon at the office we'd been told that several employees would be laid off. Those of us affected would be notified at week's end. I fretted over the pile of bills that had accumulated and wondered how we would manage if I lost my job. "Don't worry," my husband, Del, had insisted. But I couldn't help it. As I hugged a sofa pillow and prayed, *Lord, help me trust in your care,* I recalled a treasured memory of forty years earlier.

It was our first January together. We were so young, nineteen and twenty years old. Married for only ten months, our first baby coming in April, we had dreams and plans, but none were working out.

Del had a job washing windows, but the starting salary was barely enough for us to live on. My difficult pregnancy prevented me from working. Our home was a small trailer parked in a mobile home court on the outskirts of Spokane, Washington. Sparsely furnished with a drop-leaf table, a folding chair, the backseat from a car and a small bed, the trailer had belonged to a hunter and bore the scars of many trips. It lacked a bathroom, so we had to use the shower and rest rooms in a laundry house nearby.

Nevertheless, we had managed to have a happy Christmas. We bought a little tree and trimmed it with handmade decorations and popcorn. On Christmas Eve we went to our church for the candlelight services, savoring the scent of freshly cut evergreens as we sang carols. Back home we sat on the car-seat couch, drinking hot chocolate to stay warm while we picked names for our baby.

January arrived with bitter cold and snow. Del would go off to work shivering in a light jacket and worn boots, while doctor's orders confined me to bed. Then one freezing morning shortly after Del left for work, the flame in our temperamental fuel-oil heater went out. The winds rattled our flimsy home, blowing through every crack. I put on a coat, wrapped myself in two blankets and counted the hours until Del came home.

By the time he did, I was half frozen. Immediately he began working on the old heater. The cold and our frustration set off an exchange of angry words until, at last, the only sound was Del tapping and adjusting the heater.

At 10:00 PM he finally got it going again.

For a late supper we ate boiled cabbage and stale bread. Without feeling very thankful, we bowed our heads and said grace. Tears slipped down my cheeks as I picked up my fork, forcing myself to eat. Del sat across from me, looking thin and tired. We barely said a word to each other. I knew he was worried about me and our baby. I wanted to reach out to him, to tell him everything would be okay, but I was so filled with self-pity I couldn't.

Just then we heard footsteps on the wooden crate that served as our doorstep. Who would be coming to see us at this hour?

We waited for the knock. Instead, we heard a child singing, *"Silent night, holy night, all is calm, all is bright."* The clear, sweet, pure notes came from just outside the door. It was so startling, so comforting, neither of us moved. *"Round yon virgin mother and child. Holy infant so tender and mild."* The cold, our meager dinner, the ramshackle trailer, none of it mattered. We listened to the angelic tones that floated through the night air. *"Sleep in heavenly peace."*

Then there was silence. Del and I jumped up at the same time, with the same thought: *Why was a child out so late in the cold?*

Del opened the door carefully so as not to scare whoever it was. Light spilled onto the wooden step. Fresh snow covered it and an untouched white blanket buried the path to our door. Where was the child?

Without even grabbing our coats, we raced outside and walked around our trailer and the homes nearby. Most of them were dark; everyone was inside, asleep. Driven indoors by the cold, we returned and stood in the middle of the trailer amazed.

We had both heard the unmistakable sound of feet on our wooden step and a child's voice lifted in song. Life was hard at the moment, but we knew we would be okay. Del opened his arms and held me close. "We've got each other," he said, "and someone is watching over us."

A few days later Del's supervisor gave him a raise and offered him overtime hours until spring. The additional income allowed us to move to a small house, and when the baby arrived we managed our medical bills just fine.

Now, four decades later, I began to take stock. We had a beautiful family and a fine home—God had given us so much to be thankful for. We would make it through this crisis, even if I lost my job. All I needed was to have faith.

I went back to the window, opened the drapes and looked at the sky. The clouds were drifting apart, letting the stars shine through, and in my mind I could hear the pure voice of a child singing on the doorstep about heavenly peace, just waiting for me to let it in.

You Can (Usually) Count on Me

JENNIFER MILLER

*M*iss Organization—that's me. My desk calendar was always up-to-date, with all my appointments printed clearly in the boxes: Attend my son's choral program on Monday, take our new kitten to the vet for shots on Wednesday, make brownies for the kids' bake sale on Thursday. Checked and double-checked. When people were counting on me I wasn't about to let them down!

On Sunday night I looked at my desk calendar to preview my schedule for the week. My eye fell on the Friday that had just passed.

In the box I'd carefully written: play piano at Maple Lawn. I had completely forgotten my monthly appointment at the nursing home! "I feel terrible!" I told my husband, Dale, who worked as development director at the home. "How could I have forgotten those lovely people?"

"Everybody makes mistakes, hon," Dale said. "And no one at Maple Lawn even mentioned it to me. I'm sure they understand."

Still I felt terrible. I remembered how happy the elderly folks had been at the last sing-along. The nurses escorted them into the community center, some in wheelchairs, some using walkers or canes. Others made it slowly, all on their own. Everyone settled into a seat and leafed through the hymnbooks, requesting old favorites. "Let's do 'In the Garden,'" a woman called out. The others agreed. When we'd finished, a gentleman raised his hand.

"'There Is a Fountain,'" he requested.

"Sure," I called. We turned to it in our hymnbooks. All the residents sang with gusto, and I knew how much they were looking forward to our next get-together. *God, I know you were with those people when I forgot them.* I just hoped they knew that. I'd never forgive myself for letting them down.

I thought about it all weekend. Before Dale left for work Monday morning, he promised to talk to Marj, the volunteer coordinator, and explain what had happened.

"Were the folks at Maple Lawn very disappointed?" I asked Dale when he got back from work that evening.

He shook his head, looking confused. "I told Marj how sorry you were for missing the sing-along, and she said you shouldn't worry. The replacement you sent did a fine job."

"Replacement?" I said. "I didn't send any replacement."

"That's what I told Marj," Dale said. "She said a woman showed up right on time, sat down at the piano and started to play. Marj was sure you'd sent her to take your place."

A lot of people count on me. And I know I can count on God. He will never let me down.

Early Morning Announcement

LORAINE STAYER

his is a hard night for me, Lord. I was saying my evening prayers, looking out the window, watching a tree sway back and forth. I should've been long asleep like my husband, but how could I relax? Our daughter Miriam was at a hospital two states away, about to give birth to her first child.

Like any other grandmother-to-be, I was filled with excitement and butterflies. I wished I knew how she was doing moment by moment, but since Miriam and her husband follow a strict Jewish tradition, they don't use the phone on holy days. *Just my luck it's a holy day!* I thought. And I'd certainly pestered the nurses enough. I'd just have to wait it out and have faith that everything would work out okay.

I sat down on my bed. *God,* I whispered, *give me strength and peace of mind to fall asleep tonight.* By morning I would learn all about my beautiful new grandbaby and hear about the birth from my daughter. What would it be, a boy or a girl? Just so mother and baby were healthy, that's what mattered.

I slipped under the covers and glanced at the answering machine. *Don't even look at it,* I told myself. I closed my eyes and took a deep breath. . . .

But what was this? I found myself sitting in my dining room. I had to be dreaming. That was it. But everything seemed so real. Suddenly an angel appeared before me. There was no question as to his nature. He had no wings but wore a yarmulke. A long, bright scroll unfurled in his hands, and he sang out, "You have a grandson."

I woke up with a start and looked around the dark bedroom. The clock radio read 5:00 AM. My husband slept soundly beside me. I pulled the covers up to my chin, thinking how tremendously beautiful that voice was.

"The voice of an angel," I murmured. Was his announcement true? Somehow I felt that mother and baby were fine. As I drifted off to sleep again, I heard the phone ring. The answering machine picked up. The same wonderful voice again sang, *"You have a grandson."*

How nice of the hospital to call, I thought. I was elated. In my sleepy state, I supposed all good news sounded as if it came from an angel!

When I woke up later that morning I checked the message. There was no message at all. I looked down at the red, flashing zero. Of course there's no message, I realized. You were dreaming. Since when do hospitals leave singing messages on people's machines?

Soon we learned my healthy grandson had been born at exactly five o'clock in the morning. My daughter was doing just fine. Grandmother, never better! Surely this had been a holy day.

In the Hollow of His Hand

MELANIE EMORY

The summer Melanie was seventeen, she played the piano at a North Carolina camp meeting where God dramatically touched her life and where she committed herself anew to him: *I'll serve you the rest of my life.* Here's the "next chapter" of her story—what happened that autumn.

One Sunday morning in September, Mama wanted to go to the church of a friend of hers, the Church of God in Woodfin, about twenty miles away from our home in the hollow that nestles Mills River, North Carolina.

I'd never been in this church before. As we walked in late, during a congregational song, I glanced around the large sanctuary. An impressive wooden cross hung on the wall behind the pulpit. And an impressive young man stood in the back row of the choir. I couldn't take my eyes off him... his broad smile, blue eyes, dark curly hair. During the sermon I had to force myself to concentrate on the message and not on the tenor wearing the red tie. *God, forgive me for being so distracted,* I prayed. *And help me pay attention.*

It's as if the preacher himself heard my prayer. In the middle of his message, he abruptly interrupted himself. Suddenly, he had *everyone's* attention. "This is very unusual for me. But the Lord is telling me to say that there are two people in this congregation whose destiny will be fulfilled this day."

The words darted to my spirit. I nudged my mother's arm. "Mama, he's talking to me."

She raised her eyebrows, acknowledging what I said but also telling me to *hush.*

O Lord, what's this *about?* I wondered. *Whatever it means, I'm ready.*

After the service, before we even got out into the aisle, that young smiling man walked up to me. He looked right into my eyes as he reached to shake my hand. "Hello, I'm Philip Emory," he said.

I introduced myself and my mother, and Philip asked if we'd be able to come back for the evening service.

At six we were there, and Philip greeted us again after the service. "I know you're going to think I'm very forward, but I'd like to take you and your mother out to dinner." Nothing fancy—the Pizza Hut in Asheville.

Mama smiled at me and then at him. Yes, she said, we'd be delighted. At the restaurant I picked at one piece of pizza. I still couldn't keep my eyes off this young man. This just wasn't like me. And Mama was acting out of character also. There was always a mother-hen quality about her; she was very particular about whom I was out with. But this night she agreed that Philip and I could take our time and that he could drive me home to Mills River. "I can go on ahead. You two can stay awhile."

As I toyed with that pizza, I admitted my excitement about the day. "I think it was destiny that I came to Woodfin this morning."

Philip wasn't subtle in his reply. "Well, you know it is. Didn't you hear the preacher?"

As we talked, Philip fiddled with a straw wrapper. Before we left he slid his handiwork across the table to me: He'd twisted it in the shape of a ring. "Melanie, I think we've got something here."

When he delivered me back home, I met Mama in the living room. When we were alone, I started to cry. I remember her response. "Well, young lady, you just might be Mrs. Emory one day." Was this my mother speaking? The woman I thought wanted me to live with her until I died?

I walked to my room thinking, *This must be the Lord.*

In the next month, I saw a lot of Philip. He was only nineteen, but he had a seasoned gift for preaching. An electrician by trade, he felt a call to be an evangelist.

Was it a coincidence that for years I'd felt that I would someday marry a preacher?

Was it a coincidence that he'd been praying for a wife who was a musician?

In the pulpit his words came as naturally to him as my music came to me. Was it a coincidence that we'd both been "taught by God"?

Lord, I prayed, *can it be? Can this be the future you have for me?*

God chose to send me an answer directly from the heavens. On a seventy-degree Sunday that October, Philip and I went for a drive along the colorful Blue Ridge Parkway. "Let's drive up along the river," I suggested, wanting to show Philip some countryside he'd never seen before.

In no hurry to get to the parkway, we stopped to enjoy the view at the old Baptist Church along Mills River. The white frame building deserves a page on a "Come-to-Carolina" calendar. Secluded from neighbors, hidden against the sycamore trees, its high steeple holds a silver bell that reigns over the landscape; a well-kept yard spreads down to the riverbank and surrounding woods.

There was an old homemade quilt in the car, and we spread it out over the grass near the river. After a while, our talk turned sentimental, prompting Philip to say, "Let's pray about our future and God's will." Holding hands, on our knees facing each other, we talked to God, Philip aloud and I in my spirit. I listened as Philip placed our future in God's hands. He said he wanted to serve God; he was willing to preach, even if it meant leaving the security of his trade as an electrician. "And, Father, I thank you for giving me this helpmeet."

There was no doubt in my mind that Philip and I were someday to become one and minister the gospel of Jesus Christ together.

Philip kept praying, but suddenly I was distracted. In the distance I began to hear music, beautiful music. It grew louder and louder. I looked at Philip. He had a startled look on his face. We were hearing the same music—and we were awed. The music soared and then voices, heavenly voices sang praises and blessings. Philip and I had tears in our eyes. The sound receded until finally, after maybe ten minutes, it faded out of our range. All we could hear was the rumble of the river and the mockingbirds in the woods.

In the quiet Philip took my hand. "God's given us a sign of his blessing," Philip said with great surety.

***

Philip and I waited three years before we married, on September 12, 1992, in a quaint wedding chapel in Gatlinburg, Tennessee. As I said my "I do," my thoughts went out to the heavenly choir that had blessed my future with this chosen man.

After the reception we drove to our honeymoon hideaway, a nearby mountain chalet. That evening we snuggled in front of a fireplace with flames burning brightly. As we nibbled on party food my mother had packed up for us, our conversation turned to how God's purpose for our lives could now begin. And so it did.

As we marked our second anniversary, Philip and I restored and moved into the original homeplace that his grandfather had built. It's not in Mills River but in Philip's hometown, in another hollow with just a few houses nestled in a dip between North Carolina hills.

Every morning I wake and look up across the wooded slopes. Those hills remind me that our future rests securely in the hollow of his hand.

The Magic Violin

SHONY ALEX BRAUN

'm a concert violinist, yet I find it strange that the instrument I play for people's enjoyment also figured in the two most horrific times of my life.

The first happened when I was four. Our family lived in a small town in the Romanian province of Transylvania. Papa was a jeweler, a deeply devout man who carried on his father's rabbinical traditions. Mama kept the Sabbath, lit candles when she prayed, and nurtured us six children in our faith.

One day while Mama was busy cooking, my young nursemaid walked me near the thick woods outside of town. However, in rendezvousing with her sweetheart, she forgot about me. Intrigued by the trilling of birds, I wandered into the forest. Soon I was lost. Amid towering dark trees, my fascination turned to terror. Crying hysterically, I pushed through brush and brambles to find myself in a clearing. It was a gypsy encampment of wagons and brightly painted caravans. Smoke rose from cooking fires tended by women in long, billowing dresses. One of them saw me, came over and knelt before me. "Where are you from, little one?" she asked. I cried harder.

She called to a swarthy man with a dangling gold earring. He came over carrying a violin. Lifting it to his chin, he said: "Watch now. There's a birdie inside that will hop out when I play."

As if by magic, beautiful birdsongs sounded from the violin. My tears dried. For the brief time I was with the gypsies, I was enthralled by their music.

After being delivered home, I was consumed with a passion to play the violin. Papa found a child-size instrument, and I practiced for hours every day. At age ten I played on Radio Bucharest and at thirteen was accepted to study at the Budapest Academy of Music. Then, just when life seemed most glorious, Nazi troops marched into Hungary, which had been ruling northern Transylvania. The Csendorok, local police who worked with the Nazis, rounded us Jews up in carts. Cattle cars transported us to Auschwitz, and our nightmare began. I last saw my mother holding my nine-year-old sister's hand as they walked to the gas chambers, which were disguised as showers. And there in Auschwitz I learned to shrink from the dreaded Kapos. These were vicious, hard-core convicts appointed by the SS to head work gangs. Though still prisoners, they were free to brutalize us.

We were moved from one concentration camp to another, losing loved ones along the way. By the time we were enslaved in the Kochendorf salt mines, only Papa, my brother Zoltan and I were left. My sister Violet and brothers Emil and Adolf had been shipped elsewhere. But my father, a shining example of love and goodness, would not speak ill of the Nazis. "Never be hateful toward anyone," he admonished us.

Hunger had reduced us to near animals. A Kapo eating an apple was watched fiercely. The instant he tossed away the core, a horde of inmates flew at it. Finally, I could not take the beatings and cruelties any longer. I was fourteen years old and I wanted to die. I looked at my father laboring next to me and staggered toward the electrified fence.

Knowing my thoughts, Papa gently took my arm. "Son, did you practice the Brahms violin concerto and the Kreisler composition today?"

I shook my head.

"God has given you a wonderful talent and you want to throw it away?"

Reluctantly I turned back. While swinging my hammer at the iron-hard salt, I played the music in my mind, as Papa had me do every day. When I finished, I didn't want to die.

One cold morning, my dear papa did not show up for roll call. "Find him!" roared an officer. Worn from hunger and hard work, he had overslept. As he was dragged before us, the officer bellowed: "It took ten minutes to find this dirty Jewish dog. That was ten extra minutes Germany was kept from victory!"

Zoltan and I were forced to watch while guards ferociously kicked and bludgeoned our father. I pleaded for God to save him. But Papa crumpled into the snow, blood streaming from his mouth. His lips were moving, and I leaned closer to hear his dying gasp: "*Shema Yisroel Adonai elohainu Adonai echod.*" ("Hear, O Israel, the Lord our God, the Lord is one.")

All Zoltan and I could do was wail in anguish. Then my agony turned to anger at God. How could he allow this to happen to such a saintly man? We trudged to the mines, and I decided there was no God.

That night as I slept on vermin-infested straw, Papa came to me in a dream. "Yitzhak," he said, using my Hebrew name, "God is *real*. Have faith, trust in him and you will survive!"

I awakened comforted. I knew Papa was right. But I wondered about his promise of my survival after we were moved to Dachau. Evil hung over it like a turbid cloud.

One evening an SS officer strode into our barracks holding a violin. I hadn't seen a violin in so long. "Anyone who can play will be given food," he promised. Three hands shot up, including mine. The others were older men, one in his forties, the other about twenty-five.

We were hustled to a large room and pushed before the SS commandant. A tall, steel-eyed man in jackboots slouched in a chair. A menacing attack dog sat at his side. Three hulking Kapos, each one gripping an iron pipe, stood nearby. The commandant pointed his stick at the oldest prisoner, who was handed the violin.

"Play something," the commandant ordered in a bored tone.

The man tuned the instrument and began to play. His first notes were shaky, but soon he was playing Bach's Chaconne, Sonata No. 6 beautifully. When the final note died, the SS man barked, *"Scheusslich!"* ("Awful!") He waved at one of the Kapos, who lunged forward and viciously brought the pipe down on the violinist's head. I realized we were there for sadistic entertainment.

The body was dragged away and the second prisoner shoved forward. His face was ashen and the violin shook so in his hands that he could not play a straight note. The SS officer sneered, "You want me to give you food for *that?*" He motioned and two Kapos began kicking and beating him to death. In the commotion I bolted for the door, but another guard caught me and thrust the violin into my arms. I had never played a full-size instrument before. Trembling, I tried to focus. I had planned to play a sonatina by Dvořák or a composition by Kreisler. But my mind went blank.

"Spiel!" said the SS man, ordering me to play.

I lifted the violin to my chin, praying: *O God, how does the sonatina start? How does the Kreisler piece begin?*

"Play, *Schweinhund!*"

My fingers were so weakened by starvation I could barely curve them around the fingerboard, much less press the strings. My body turned to water as one of the Kapos eagerly advanced, raising his iron pipe.

As I stood there waiting for the pipe to strike my skull, a powerful force took hold of me. My right and left hands began to move in perfect unison without conscious effort on my part. Beautiful music poured out of my violin, like the birds that had flown out of the gypsy's that day long ago. I was playing Johann Strauss's "Blue Danube Waltz." The idea of playing that piece had not entered my mind. I had never played it before, nor had I ever seen the music. I knew immediately God was protecting me; his angel was guiding my hands.

I continued playing. All eyes were on the SS officer. But instead of signaling to the Kapo, he began humming the melody and tapping its rhythm with his fingers. When my bow swept out the last note, the commandant growled: "*Sehr gut!* Give him the food."

But I had already gained my reward: The strong certainty that whether I survived Dachau or not, God would always be with me, his angels guiding me.

Rosa's Solo

ROSA G. SANCHEZ

arly on a cold and rainy Christmas morning a few years back, I was busy wrapping presents and making tamales for our traditional family dinner at my mother's. The telephone rang. "Merry Christmas," I said, picking up.

"Good morning, Rosa. It's Angelita." Angelita was the secretary at our church. "Sorry to bring sad news, especially on Christmas Day," she said, "but Mr. Jaramillo passed away. Could you sing at the wake tonight?"

My heart went out to the Jaramillo family. I knew what it was like to lose someone during the holidays. My own brother Alfredo had died at Christmastime eighteen years ago. He was only thirty-nine. The sudden loss left a hole in my life. I hadn't spent a Christmas since without feeling an underlying sadness. "Of course I'll sing, Angelita. And I'll try to find someone to sing with me." I didn't like singing alone. *How in the world can I find someone on Christmas Day?* I wondered.

I opened the church directory to make some calls. I started with my friend Carmen, but her entire family was visiting. I called Rosa, but she was out of town. Angie was already singing with the community choir. Ezequiel was ill, and Alejandra was giving a party. There was no one to help me.

As a last resort, I asked my husband. "Honey, will you sing with me at Mr. Jaramillo's wake tonight?"

"I can't carry a tune," Bernie said. "I'd knock you off-key." He was right and I knew it. And so it was settled. I would be singing all alone, without even an organ to accompany me.

That afternoon Bernie, our two kids and I went to my mother's house for a traditional Mexican Christmas feast. After dinner we opened presents. As evening grew near, my stomach did somersaults. *Dear Lord, I want to praise you properly on this holy day. Let me sing my best to help ease the pain of Mr. Jaramillo's family and friends.* I left my mother's house and made my way to the funeral home.

The building was full of people who had gathered to pay their last respects. Not everyone could fit into the small chapel, and some people had to stand in the hallway. This large turnout would be a comfort to the Jaramillo family, I hoped. Yet I remembered how seeing the many people who attended my brother's wake had not brought me peace. Not when he had died so young. I hadn't been able to sing songs of praise in his honor. I hoped that I would be able to do it for Mr. Jaramillo.

The crowd fell silent as I stepped up to the podium. "We are gathered here to pray," I said, "for the soul of José Jaramillo, our brother, and for his family and friends, who mourn his loss." After the first prayers I began to sing "Ave Maria." No one joined in. All I could hear was my own too-strident voice. I tried to soften my tone, to sing as perfectly as I possibly could. The Jaramillo family was counting on me. *Lord, inspire me.*

The words coming out of my mouth became quieter, yet they filled the chapel and echoed into the hallway. My voice took on a tender pitch. I was surprised by its lovely sound. In all my life I'd never sung so well!

I took a deep breath before launching into the next verse. Then . . . wait . . . did I hear other voices singing along with mine? "Ave Maria" filled the room. A choir of angels could not have done better. I thought I heard instruments—a harp, a flute, a trumpet—but where were they coming from?

I looked about the chapel. No one was singing. My voice alone created the music. No instruments played. After each group of prayers I sang another hymn—and a glorious chorus joined me. With every song, my confidence grew. I found my voice. I sang with all my heart, for Mr. Jaramillo and for me. And as I sang, the sadness I always felt this time of year started to fade. There was no longer any room in my heart for it. I was filled with joy.

And I was filled with praise for the loving God who held me in his arms and held my brother just a little closer.

4

DELIVERING MERCY

Angels descending bring from above
Echoes of mercy, whispers of love.
—FANNY CROSBY

The woman who wrote these lines had been blind since infancy—the result of a doctor's incompetent treatment. Despite her limitations, she inspired generations with her many song lyrics, thanking God for his mercy. "This is my story, this is my song: praising my Savior all the day long."

Our band of angels delivering mercy is led by Archangel Michael, who is revered in the Italian city of Rome not as a warrior but for his role in stopping the devastation of a sixth-century plague.

How did I respond to these stories? By being more appreciative of kindnesses. Last night I left my reading glasses at a restaurant. This morning a friend brought them to my door. The mercy may have been delivered by a mere mortal, but my gratitude flies beyond earth, into the heavens.

Hero Michael

JOSEPH CALDWELL

*A*gain and again during the eight years I was a pupil at St. Michael School in Milwaukee, Wisconsin, I was drawn to a large photograph at the head of the stairs in the main hall. It was the school's patron, the archangel Michael, wings outspread, sword in hand, armored against the enemy. Michael was an everyday presence at the top of the stairs, faithful and unconquerable, the warrior angel, guardian of us all. Where did his strength come from?

In time I learned the origin of the picture: a statue that topped the battlements of Castel Sant'Angelo, the papal fortress in Rome. With his drawn sword, Michael was guarding the city and giving fair warning to any invader that all opposition was doomed. After all, Michael was wielding the sword that had driven the Angel of Light, Lucifer himself, from highest heaven for his prideful attempt to make himself equal to Almighty God.

After college and a stint in the Air Force, I moved to New York to become a writer, where I was able to indulge my enthusiasm for opera. One memorable evening at the old Met, lo and behold, there, in the third act of *Tosca,* looming over the entire set—of the ramparts of Castel Sant'Angelo—was the statue of my childhood hero Michael. He was even stronger, more glorious, here on the opera house stage. His name translated from the Hebrew means "Who is like God." It seemed that night that I could almost read his resounding answer: "No one is like God!" inscribed on the blade of his drawn sword. *What a statue this must be to see in person!*

My first novel won the Rome Prize in Literature, which meant I would have a year in the city often identified by a picture of Castel Sant'Angelo. During my stay as a fellow at the American Academy in Rome, I continued my writing, but just as important, I availed myself of the cultural, spiritual, historical and quotidian riches that are Rome's legacy.

The other fellows at the academy included classicists, architects, painters, sculptors, composers and art historians. This meant that when I ventured down the Janiculum Hill into the city of Rome, I often had as a guide and mentor a highly informed fellow peer.

It was late autumn. I was walking down the Lungotevere, the roadway along the Tiber embankments. The river itself was high from a rainstorm the night before, but the water was calm. The air had a clarity only a crisp autumn day can provide. At my side was John Scott, an exceptional art historian, noted even then for his erudition, his interpretive skills and his enduring pleasure in shared knowledge. We were on our way to the Vatican Museum.

At a turn in the river, just before the street that led to the museum, was Castel Sant'Angelo. As always, Michael captured my eye. The statue bestowed some sense of glory to an otherwise gloomy fortress. To lay claim to my lifelong association with the angel, I said rather loftily to John, "It really thrills me every time I see Michael there, drawing his sword, protector of the battlements, defying anyone to come near. An impressive warning if ever there was one."

John stopped in his tracks. I turned to see what was wrong. His open mouth defined the phrase "slack-jawed." His eyes had lost their ability to blink.

"What?" I asked, puzzled. "Do you disagree?"

"*Draw* his sword? Did you say *draw* his sword? What are you talking about?"

"Michael. There. The warrior angel. Guarding the fortress."

"Drawing his sword? Where'd you get that?"

"Just look. That's what he's doing. Getting ready to, as they say, smite the enemy."

"You're crazy. Totally crazy. Don't you know the history?"

"I know what I see."

"You don't see anything." And then, with barely controlled exasperation, John proceeded to settle my hash: The year was 590. Rome was in the throes of the plague. Pope Gregory, subsequently referred to as the Great, was leading a procession of penitents, imploring God to end the scourge. And there, in full splendor, crowning the summit of the fortress, was a vision of Michael. And the archangel was sheathing his sword. Not drawing it. Sheathing it. The penitents' prayers were answered.

Michael, warrior or no warrior, was still an "angelo," a messenger sent by God. But this time the messenger had come not as conqueror or avenger, but to deliver the message of God's mercy, of his active love in our lives—the most mighty of all God's glories. Death by plague would no longer ravage the city of Rome. The archangel's sheathed sword meant the withdrawal of death, the renewal of life, the coming of mercy. That was the source of Michael's strength.

All I could say to John was, "Oh." What I didn't say was that the thrill I had always felt at the sight of the statue, at the thought of the angel, had not diminished. It had grown, intensified to exhilaration. I had been guarded not by the warrior but by the Angel of Mercy. It had taken a long time, years upon years, but I had finally gotten the message.

Closer Than I Knew

MILLIE GARCIA

I loved to climb trees as a young girl in Puerto Rico. I was called Milagros then, and I lived with my grandmother while my mother and brother tried to make a life in los Estados Unidos, in New York. I was lonely sometimes, yes, but climbing a tree always made me feel better, and I had so many—mango, papaya, coconut palm and sea grape. The *quenepa* was my favorite. It was the tallest of all. Scrambling to a perch among the topmost leaves, I'd reach out my hand as far as I could and shut my eyes. "It's me, Milagros," I'd say. "I know you're there, God." He was as real to me then as the strong *quenepa* branches that held me up.

I kept this memory after I joined my mother and brother in New York. Everything changed in New York, even my name. I missed the forest and the shelter of my *quenepa*. All I had were the tall buildings and the dirty streets. In this city it seemed impossible to believe God would be there if I reached out for him. Still, I tried, especially in 1997. In my twenties, as a part-time student trying to get my GED, I was expecting a child. I felt so alone. The baby's father had left me. I went to school every day, miserable. *Milagros,* I said to myself, using my old name, *how can you take care of a baby? You can't even take care of yourself.*

I talked to God every day, even walking to class. People stared at me as if I were crazy, but I didn't care. "Why do I have to go through this?" I asked. "I'm not ready, Lord." I often sat in the park behind the school looking up through the trees, hoping for answers. "Why must I have this baby?" No answers came.

One June afternoon I dragged my feet on the way to class, my mood as heavy as the extra weight I carried. I didn't want to go to school. I didn't want the baby. Lost in my thoughts, I stepped off a curb and into the street. A car roared toward me. I couldn't move. "Milagros!" someone called. "*Cuidao!*" "Be careful." A hand grabbed the neck of my sweatshirt. With a hard jerk I was pulled back onto the curb just as the car sped by. I turned to thank the person who had saved me. I was alone. What about the hand I felt? God had touched me. I knew that for certain. And I knew I was meant to have my baby.

I learned everything I could about being a mother. I read books and went to Lamaze classes. Then, at the hospital on my delivery day, I gasped and dropped to the floor. My mother ran for help. Seconds later the room was full of nurses. They snapped an oxygen mask over my mouth and stuck an IV in my arm. Someone said, "She's losing the baby." I reached wildly into the air.

God, I begged, *give me your hand!*

A strong hand grasped mine. At my side was a handsome African-looking man wearing a shirt and tie. He was the doctor in charge. The nurses lifted me onto a gurney and wheeled it out of the room. The doctor held my hand as we hurried down the hall. I had the strangest sensation, almost as if someone had reached right into my body. Panicked, I looked at the doctor. "Don't worry," he whispered. "I'm massaging your baby's heart." I closed my eyes, breathed deeply, and suddenly I wasn't in the hospital anymore. I was in a tropical forest, surrounded by *quenepa* trees. I opened my eyes. I was about to go into the operating room. The doctor was still with me.

I drifted off, but I heard the doctor say, "Go back. Your baby needs you. His name is Matthew, because he's a gift from God." After the C-section the nurses showed me my son. *He's here,* I said to myself. *I can rest now.*

Matthew had to stay in the ICU for observation. He looked beautiful to me, despite a tube in his nose and an IV in his tiny hand.

"May I see the doctor?" I asked one of the nurses.

"Which doctor?" she said. I described the man who'd held my hand. The doctor in a shirt and tie. She shook her head. "There were only nurses in your room," she said. Once again, I knew God had touched me.

Matthew will soon be six, and I plan to take him to Puerto Rico. We will stare up through the branches of my *quenepa,* and I'll tell him what I believe: If you climb as high as you can and reach out your hand, God will touch you with his.

Trash!

MARY ANN GARDNER

ightning was outside barking nonstop. Our sable-and-white Border collie was beautiful all right but definitely not shy about announcing our guests. He barked at everything, which was fine with me. My two young sons and I had been alone for the past week, but I felt safe with Lightning around.

"Okay, Lightning," I called. "I hear you." I looked out the window. The movers. Eight AM, right on time. My husband, Bob, had started his new job in Kansas, so it was up to me and the boys to take care of every last detail of our move from South Dakota ourselves. Once our house was empty, we'd pack up the car and meet Bob's incoming flight at the airport. Then we'd all drive to our new home to spend the next day, July Fourth, together.

I pulled out my long to-do list and felt a sense of accomplishment as I scanned the items I'd already crossed out: cancel phone service, stop paper delivery, shut off gas, transfer kids' school records, close bank accounts, empty safety deposit box. Now I put a line through "Movers arrive, 8:00 AM."

My six-year-old, James, played in the backyard while twelve-year-old Michael acted as my guy Friday. We let in the movers. "Hi. My name's Charlie," one man said. "We'll start with the living room. Okay?"

"Great," I said. "All I ask is that you finish by four thirty. That's when the carpet cleaners will get here."

As Charlie and his crew emptied a room, I'd clean it behind them. I was amazed at how much junk I was finding: the boys' old school papers behind their dressers, stray socks on a closet shelf and even an unfinished sandwich under one of the beds. As I filled a trash bag, Michael would haul it out to the garage along with empty boxes and any other junk that would not be moving with us.

By lunch I'd crossed "living room," "master bedroom" and "boys' rooms" off my list. The movers took a short break.

Right after lunch I heard Lightning barking his head off. That must be the carpet cleaners. *They're early!* I ran to the window. "Oh no," I moaned.

Charlie came up behind me. "We'll just put the rest of the furniture out on the lawn for the time being. Don't worry."

As the carpet cleaners approached the front door, Lightning kept on barking. "Hush, Lightning! They're here to help us." The cleaners started in the empty rooms, and I continued picking up behind Charlie's crew, while Michael carried out his trash-hauling duties.

By three o'clock, the carpet cleaners were finished with their work. One more item crossed off my list. *Please, Lord, don't let me forget anything.* I put our suitcases into the trunk. Everything was going great. I could finally see the end in sight. At five, Charlie's crew was done. The kids and I sat on the kitchen floor and had a cold drink.

"What are we gonna do with all the trash?" Michael said.

I almost choked on my drink. The trash! How could I have forgotten the trash? I looked into the garage at the huge pile of junk. We usually made a trip a week to the city dump, just five miles away. But the dump closed at five! Now, over the holiday weekend, our real estate agent would have to show the house to prospective buyers with a garage full of trash. *Lord, we have to be at the airport in an hour. What can I do?*

Then I heard an engine outside the house. *Who could that be?* I waited for Lightning to bark. Nothing. The engine cut off. "Somebody drove up to the garage," Michael said.

"Lightning's out there. Why isn't he barking?" I said.

A car door slammed. But no one came to the door. Then I heard muffled noises in the garage. "*Shh!*" I said to the boys. "Don't make a sound." I quickly double-bolted the door. *Where was Lightning?* I wished I hadn't cut off the phone.

"Michael, James, let's stay together." *God, please watch over us.* The car door slammed again, and the engine whirred. Michael ran to the door and looked out the peephole just in time to see our mystery visitor drive away. "It was a pickup truck!" he said. "Filled with our trash!" We ran out to the garage, and it was empty.

"Who took it?" James asked.

Lightning came out of the garage and sat at my feet. "Why didn't you bark, boy?" I asked. He just licked my hand. "I guess we'll never know who got us out of that jam."

James looked up at me and grinned. "Maybe it was an angel, Mom. Not even Lightning would bark at an angel."

I put my arm around my boys and thought of how everything had gone so right that day. Every little detail had fallen perfectly into place.

I pulled out my list, which had once seemed so important, and looked it over. Then I tore it up. I had finally realized that God has his own list, and he never forgets a thing. Not even a trash-hauling angel.

Message in the Sand

POLLY AUGENSTEIN

*U*sually I'm not an early riser, but on our beach vacation in Fort Lauderdale I was up with the sun. The flash of dawn on the water and peaceful rhythm of the waves against the shore always made me feel close to God. I pulled on my clothes, anxious to get outside and walk in the sand.

Life had seemed hard lately. My computer-consulting business kept me more busy than I sometimes wanted to be, not to mention managing the office and doing all of the bookkeeping for my husband Chuck's oil business. And then there were our teenage sons, who needed my guidance more than ever these important years. With so many responsibilities I'd been feeling overburdened, and I wanted reassurance that God was nearby to help me carry the load.

Careful not to wake Chuck and the boys, I crept out of the hotel room and made my way to the empty beach. Breaking sunlight danced on the water. Majestic waves rolled up to kiss the shore, powerful and gentle all at once, just like God. But his closeness eluded me now. It seemed almost too much to ask for a sign. How could someone so awesome care about my small life?

I walked along the water line, where shells and tiny rocks tumbled over my toes. I kicked a lump of coral. A white shell stuck up out of the sand. It was somewhat heart-shaped with a smaller red heart seemingly painted in the center. I've never seen such a shell!

I bent over to pick it up. One touch and I was filled with the most wonderful reassurance, as if God himself had whispered, "I love you, Polly."

I cupped my find in my hand and walked on. Shells of all kinds lay on the beach. What were the chances that this one was a message meant for me? Impossible. A *Y*-shaped piece of coral caught my eye. As I bent down to pick it up, I saw another piece of coral, this one shaped like an *L*, with its twin lying close beside it. *Y*, *L*, *L*—and what was that just ahead? Coral, in a doughnut shape. "Or the letter *O*," I said to myself, pondering the letters in the palm of my hand. If only I had a *P*! But there were no other coral pieces in my path. Except that one piece I kicked earlier—

I stopped short, turned around and retraced my steps. It had to be around somewhere. There, stuck in the sand. I pulled it out, brushed it off and turned it into position. A perfect letter *P*. Someone more powerful and more beautiful than the ocean wanted me to know that he cared for me by name.

Somewhere in Sudan

DENNIS CUTSHAW

Wilfred Thesiger was my favorite writer when I was in college. Born in Ethiopia in 1910 to a diplomat, Thesiger spent much of his life in Africa, first as a child and then as a soldier in World War II. When he wrote of his travels, he celebrated one thing above all else: hardship. "The harder the life, the finer the person." That was his credo. He traveled like a destitute drifter. He slept on the ground under the stars with the natives and ate their food and drink. Thesiger suffered plenty for his philosophy: almost starving to death, contracting third-world diseases, you name it. But he didn't regret a moment.

It was because of Thesiger that I decided to go on my own African adventure. It was 1961, and I was nearing the end of what should have been my senior year at Stanford University. I was twelve credits shy of graduating, but I wasn't sure what I was graduating for. I always imagined that by the time I was a senior, I'd have it all figured out. But the only thing I had figured out was I loved to read, especially Thesiger. As far as direction in my life, that was the best I could do. Africa seemed to clarify things for Thesiger; perhaps it could do the same for me.

My last semester at Stanford would have to wait. I made plans quickly and sailed from New York City to France. From there I drove from Paris to Beirut and then from Cairo to Sudan, right where my hero had most of his adventures. After reading about it for years, I'd finally made it to Africa.

Sudan was greater than all of my daydreams and romantic notions put together. The land was vast and alien, gorgeous in every sense of the word. You could feel the history, the people, places and things all around you. Thesiger always scoffed at the idea of not drinking the local water on his travels. "I've never boiled or sterilized water anywhere in my life, and I've drunk it out of every ditch and drain that I've been to," he wrote. Lifting my glass to Thesiger, I downed my first cup of local river water. Delicious.

I was on a boat on the Nile River heading to Khartoum when I started to regret that decision. My stomach groaned in pain. Then came violent cramps and nausea. When the boat pulled into a makeshift port at a small village, I stumbled off in search of a doctor. Amid a cluster of mud huts I found the only stone structure. The hospital.

An Arab doctor met me. By that time, the pain was so bad I could hardly speak. It felt like my insides were being torn apart. The doctor put me in bed and gave me some fluids. Malaria. In my feverish state, it was the only word I understood.

I was in the hospital for five days. Long silences were punctuated with brief visits from the doctor or overheard snippets of unintelligible conversation from the hallway. At first I could barely sit up, but eventually I gained my strength back. When I could stand up by myself I got dressed. From the look of things, this was a free clinic. And a good thing too. I'd been headed to Khartoum to pick up some much-needed money from the Western Union. How would I get there now?

"I am a long way from Stanford," I said aloud as I opened the door of the hospital and stepped out into the blinding sun. I was broke and alone in a part of the world I was completely unfamiliar with. I'd come to Africa in search of clarification, but things were more cloudy than they'd ever been. I worried I'd be stranded. I walked toward the train station, not knowing what I'd do once I got there.

The train station was hardly more than a platform with tracks next to it. I looked down the way for the train I heard in the distance. But how would I get aboard? I had no money and couldn't speak the language. *I'm just as stuck here as I was at Stanford,* I thought.

Out of the corner of my eye I saw a well-dressed, aristocratic-looking black man approaching me. "Can I be of some service?" he asked in flawless English.

Stunned, I explained that I was stranded. He pulled out his wallet. "The fare to Khartoum," he said, handing me some bills. He raised his hand before I could speak up, turned and walked away as the train pulled into the station. Confused as ever, I dropped into a seat on the train. I'd get my money in Khartoum and continue on my journey. But I'd continue it back at Stanford. Just when it felt like I was really stuck, suddenly I was on my way again. *Maybe it was just the same at school,* I thought. *When the right moment comes, God will point me on my way and I'll know what to do with my future.*

That train ride was the first leg of my journey back. I made it home safe, graduating the following year. But not before John F. Kennedy spoke at my campus about a new program, the Peace Corps. I was one of the first to join and shipped down to South America. I've never gotten stuck as badly as that time in Sudan. Partly because I've learned that God wants me to keep on moving. Ever since, I've been on my way.

Sometimes He Sends Two

BARBARA LOHR

Narth Carolina's Outer Banks was a popular vacation spot in the summer, but my husband, Jeff, and I preferred to make our visits during the off-season. Miles and miles of sandy beach, wide-open water and not a soul in sight. That's all I saw as Jeff and I walked along the shore. It brought us back year after year. The water was even warm enough to swim in. Not that I ever did. Sitting in the sun with a good book was more my speed. I'd had swimming lessons growing up and could dog-paddle my way from one end of a pool to the other, but the ocean was different. Especially this stretch of the Atlantic. The Outer Banks was known for riptides, strong currents that hid under calm water and pulled swimmers out to sea. Neither Jeff nor I had ever found one in all our years of vacationing here, and that was fine by me. Even an experienced swimmer like Jeff could get in trouble with one.

He pulled off his T-shirt. "I'm going in. Just to that sandbar and back."

"Have fun. I'll sit here and enjoy the view." Jeff kicked off his sandals and gave me a wave as he raced into the water. He cut through the ocean in smooth, even strokes. I got myself settled on the sand.

Behind me a row of beach houses stood empty, waiting for the summer crowds. They wouldn't have the beach to themselves like we did now.

I squinted out at the water, sparkling in the bright morning sun. Jeff didn't seem to be making such steady progress anymore. Either he was moving slower, or that sandbar was moving farther out to sea. He ought to turn around and come in. I stretched my neck. *What was he doing?* Jeff stopped swimming, but he didn't turn around. Was he treading water? Resting? I sat up to get a better look and a shock of fear went through me. Jeff was struggling, fighting the waves! *Riptide!* I thought. The familiar word was suddenly attached to a terrible reality.

Jeff's head went under the water. My hand flew to my chest. I jumped up, my feet planted in the sand, my eyes searching for Jeff. His head broke the surface. His hand shot up in the air. Was he signaling me? He went under again. *Lord, he's in trouble!*

I stumbled into the water. But what was I going to do? I'd never waded in past my knees. Now I was going to swim my struggling husband back to shore? I'd end up drowning him for sure. Even I knew the number-one rule for a swimmer caught in a riptide: Don't panic. I would be a detriment to Jeff.

"Help me," I whispered to the miles of empty beach. "Help us!" I pleaded at the long row of empty rentals. It was useless to scream. If only I could will someone into existence! *Dear God, help!*

I splashed forward into the water—and turned to look behind me. Two men had appeared out of nowhere. "My husband!" I managed, pointing. The younger man splashed into the water. He made his way to Jeff like a champion swimmer. The older man stayed with me. I breathed easier just knowing he was there by my side.

I saw the young man grab Jeff around the chest. With what looked like no effort at all, the man pulled him toward shore! The riptide was certainly no match for this swimmer.

Jeff dog-paddled to help them along and they made quick progress. At last they reached shore. Jeff collapsed at my feet, coughing and gasping for air. "Jeff!" I said, kneeling down beside him.

"I'm all right," he spat out.

I held him to me. "Thank you, God, for sending these men to save my husband!" Jeff and I sat there, huddled on the sand, safe in each other's embrace until his breathing became regulated. Once it sank in that he was okay, I felt embarrassed by our emotional display. I hadn't even thanked the strangers! "Please forgive me—"

But when I pulled away from Jeff and looked up, both men were gone. I got to my feet and looked around. "Now how could they have disappeared so fast?" I said to Jeff. "And that's how fast they showed up too."

Jeff took my hand, and we headed to our place to pack up. After such a scare, we were eager to get back home.

At church on Sunday, the pastor gave a surprising sermon. "Angels aren't confined to the heavenly realm," he said. "They are all around us. On earth every day, doing God's work." I thought of the men who appeared out of nowhere. I turned to Jeff. He looked at me.

Could it be . . . ? Jeff read my mind. "Definitely," he whispered.

"But why would God send two?" Jeff said afterward. "He only needed to send one angel to save my life."

Then it hit me: We'd been saying prayers of gratitude for God saving Jeff's life, but that was thanking God for half a miracle. He'd sent an angel to save my husband from drowning, but he had also sent a second angel to comfort me during Jeff's ordeal.

Jeff and I have faced other troubles since that day. Yet whenever challenges arise, all I have to do is remember those men on the beach. I know God is taking care of us. A God who cares enough to send that second angel when one would do.

5

BRINGING HOPE

Perhaps the Creator himself needed hope in order to bring the
universe into being and then have the patience to see it through.
—ARTHUR GORDON, *A Song Called Hope*

"The God of hope." It's a phrase straight out of the writings of the apostle Paul, who prayed that "the God of hope" would fill his Roman readers "with all joy and peace in believing, so that by the power of the Holy Spirit you may abound in hope" (Romans 15:13 RSV). Paul tied hope to joy and peace and power—connections I see in the stories that follow, starting with hope sweeping into the life of Lou Dean.

Hope ushers us into the future—the next hour, the next task, the next prayer, the next page . . . Turn and read, in hope of joy.

Hope and the Hummingbirds

LOU DEAN

Summer for me meant the return of my hummingbirds. I called them mine because I'd hung feeders around the porch for fifteen years, and I was certain some of the same birds came back year after year. They gave me a sense of continuity, something I could count on.

One summer I needed the bright flutter of wings more than ever. In three years I'd lost three important people in my life—my brother, my mom and a dear friend. *Why live at all, if we're just going to die?* I wondered. The thought wouldn't let go of me. It robbed me of joy and left me feeling bleak and hopeless. Death seemed to blot out the sun itself.

The hummingbirds were late that year. Finally one afternoon while I sat on the porch bench listening to the wind chimes, I heard the familiar buzz and whir of wings. "You didn't forget me," I said. The birds flitted among the flowers and drank from the feeders. They were as beautiful as ever. Vibrations from their beating wings charged the summer air. But not even my hummingbirds could lift my spirits.

Then one morning, sweeping the porch, I saw a hummer lying at my feet, still as stone. I crouched down beside him. Another death. I wept like there was no tomorrow.

God knew when every creature fell. How could a loving God bear the sadness? How could I?

I gently scooted the bird into the dustpan with the broom. "You'll rest under the lilacs," I said wearily. The hummers loved to buzz there. Walking toward the bushes, a lump hardened in my throat. I wanted to pray, but for what? *Lord, I need you. Show me how to go on.*

Right now I had a job to do, sad as it was. I stared at the hummingbird. Yet again, death was the winner. Then I looked closer. The bird's chest was moving—just barely—but moving nonetheless. "You're alive!" I gasped, sweeping him onto the dustpan.

I hurried into the house with him and searched through my nature books to find what to do. Hummingbirds, I learned, required a huge number of calories. "So that's why you buzz around the feeders all the time," I said. I got an eyedropper from an old medicine bottle, washed and sterilized it, and then filled it with nectar. I hesitated to touch my tiny friend, but there was no other way. Carefully, I transferred him from the dustpan to the palm of my hand. He weighed no more than a breath.

"Don't be afraid." I tried dropping the liquid toward him, but he moved his long, slender beak away. Then it came to me. "You need to be upright to drink." Taking one of the feeders from the eave of the porch, I set it on the table and held the bird so he could punch his beak down into the nectar. "C'mon. You can do it." He made one feeble attempt and then went limp in my hand.

Instantly I got an idea. I put the hummingbird and feeder in an empty shoe box, and balanced the box on the porch railing, just below a hanging feeder. I sat quietly on the porch bench and waited. For a few moments, only the warm summer breeze played the wind chimes. But then I heard the whir of wings as hummers approached the hanging feeder. The injured hummingbird immediately stirred at the sound of his friends. His head came up, and he fluttered his wings, trying to fly. He managed to land on one of the perches of the feeder in the box. Another bird joined him. The healthy bird dipped his beak into the feeder. To my amazement, my little friend dipped his beak too. When the other bird flew away, my bird sat on his newfound perch, still weak but upright. "Good boy!" After a few minutes, first one bird and then another jetted down to the box and helped himself to the nectar. My hummer drank along with them.

He flipped his wings into gear, hovering inches above the box. "Don't fall. Don't fall," I whispered, holding my breath. He landed safely back on his perch. Second launch, same scenario. Later, on the third try, he went straight up above his perch, out of the box and into the trees. "Hurrah!" The hummer had reached for life, and he'd found it.

I would reach too. Because death never wins, not really. My mother, my brother and my friend were with God, and their love was ever alive in my heart. Hope had come back to me, carried on the tiniest of wings.

Diving In

MARIE D. JONES

Saturday mornings growing up I could hardly wait for the sun to rise because I knew weekends meant time with Nana and Poppy, my grandparents on my father's side. They lived in Connecticut, just an hour's drive away from our house in New York, but being with them was like being in a different world. A magical world of "let's-just-pick-up-and-go" road trips, card games in their camper, harvests of fruit from the trees and grapevines twining around their yard.

Best of all were summer weekends—sometimes turning into whole weeks—at Nana and Poppy's cabin on Lake Ashuelot in the New Hampshire woods. The cabin was right on the lake, its deck perched on stilts like the legs of some huge, awkward wading bird. I loved winding my way through the woods, looking for animal tracks amid the dirt and fallen pine needles. Deer, raccoon, rabbit . . . it was always a thrill to find a paw print that matched the drawings in my *Field Guide to North American Mammals*. I loved the barbecues we had almost every evening. I loved falling asleep to the sound of the water lapping against the deck. And I loved swimming in the lake with Nana.

The water temperature, even in summer, took some getting used to, so we could have slipped into the lake from the deck or tiptoed in from the dirt bank beside the cabin. But both options were the easy way out (well, in) as far as my grandmother and I were concerned. We liked to climb to the highest of the rocky ledges around the other side of the cabin and dive in from there. For a moment we'd stand poised on the ledge, our toes curled around the lip of the rock, our arms extended over our heads. Then Nana would glance over at me, the look in her eyes daring me to make the leap first.

Splash! Splash! Brrr! The chill would send me shooting to the surface. I'd poke my head out of the water, teeth chattering, and see Nana flash me a smile. "C'mon, Marie, let's get warmed up!" Then she'd set off for the cabin, moving through the water with a smooth, steady stroke. I'd follow in her wake, and by the time we got to where I could feel the muddy lake floor squish between my toes, I wouldn't feel cold anymore. It was hard to remember that Nana was actually my dad's mom because most of the time she acted like she was just as much of a kid as I was.

"How did you get to be such a good swimmer?" I asked her one afternoon when we were sitting on the deck together, drying off in the warm sun after one of our dips.

"It's in my blood," Nana replied. "You should have seen my mother, your great-gram Margie Grato. Now she was an excellent swimmer."

I'd heard stories about Great-gram Margie. How she came to America as a child "on the boat" from her native Naples, Italy. How she settled in Bridgeport, Connecticut, on Capitol Avenue. How she liked to cook up huge Italian feasts for the family.

"Great-gram Margie used to swim in this very same water," my grandmother told me. "It was as cold back in those days as it is now, and sometimes people—mostly tourists who didn't know any better—would go for a dip and find themselves in trouble."

"What happened to them, Nana?" I asked.

"Nothing, Marie," she said. "Not if your great-grandmother could help it. She was a little lady, but strong—strong enough to rescue much bigger people from drowning. Once she spotted a man in the distance barely keeping his head above water. Looked like his muscles were cramping up on him. Great-gram Margie jumped in the lake and headed straight for him. He'd slipped completely under by the time she reached him, so she dove beneath him and pushed him to the surface. The man was twice her size, but she towed him back to shore, wrapping her body around his to keep him warm all the way."

"Wow, Great-gram Margie was some lifeguard!" I exclaimed, leaning my head on Nana's shoulder.

When I was in my teens my family moved to southern California, and I never stopped missing those weekends with Nana. From time to time we went back to visit. After Nana and Poppy passed away, though, there was less reason for me to travel back East.

It wasn't until I was in my early thirties, making a living as a freelance writer, that I decided to return to the cabin for an extended stay. Ideas for a book had been percolating in my mind for months, but I couldn't seem to get started on the manuscript. It was as if I was afraid whatever I put down on paper wouldn't measure up to the big ideas I'd been carrying around. I thought a few weeks in the peace and quiet of the New Hampshire woods might bring me the inspiration I desperately needed.

That first night back at the cabin on Lake Ashuelot, I took a deep breath of the pine-tinged air. *I've come to the right place*, I thought before being lulled to sleep by the soft lapping of the water. I woke the next day intending to write, but I found myself putting my notebook aside yet again and pulling on my bathing suit instead. *A swim will invigorate me*, I rationalized, walking out to the dirt bank leading to the lake. The sun broke through the morning clouds with a promise of warmth, so I did something I hadn't done in years.

I went around the other side of the cabin and climbed to the highest ledge above the water. Curling my toes around the lip of the rock, I closed my eyes. I imagined Nana right there beside me, daring me to dive in.

I knew as soon as my body hit the water I'd made a big mistake. It was as if the lake had grown a thousand icy tentacles and every one of them was grabbing at me. I felt my muscles go tight, cramping up before I could take even a couple of strokes toward shore.

It was only fifty feet off. I had to keep swimming. I just had to. But I couldn't. My limbs felt frozen. All I could do was try frantically to keep my head above the surface. The dirt bank seemed so far away. Too far.

"God," I gasped, "please send someone to help me!"

I felt a strange, almost molten warmth envelop me, infusing my aching muscles with energy. Had I hit a warm pocket in the lake? I started to dog paddle, afraid that I would swim into frigid water again but more afraid that I would never make it to shore if I didn't move while I could.

Yet as I swam, pulling closer to the bank with each stroke, the warmth kept me in its embrace. As soon as my toes touched the muddy bottom, I stood. Another mistake. My feet got sucked into the mud, its grip as tenacious as that of the cold had been. I fought to lift my legs, leaning into that warm embrace, trying to draw strength from it.

That's when I distinctly felt a pair of hands wrap around my ankles and, with one strong, sure push, boost me out of the mud toward shore. Soon I stumbled up the dirt bank. For a long time, I stood there shivering, hoping the sun would warm me, and stared out at the lake, waiting for my rescuer to climb out of the water. But no one ever did.

Later that day, I sat inside the cabin, unable to write a word of the book I'd come here to work on, unable to think of anything but making sense of my near-drowning.

Frustrated, I put down my notebook and looked out the window at the water. Right then Nana's story about her mother's daring lake rescues came back to me. All at once I understood what had happened to me that morning in the icy waters of Ashuelot. Hadn't I asked God for help? Who better for him to send to my rescue than the angel of the lake, a lifeguard extraordinaire just like Great-gram Margie?

I picked up my notebook and opened it to a clean page. I was ready at last to plunge into my writing, knowing that if I got stuck, God would send an angel to my rescue.

The Old Watch

L. WELLINGTON MILLER

The night was quiet as I sat at my desk with some bookkeeping. I glanced over at the glass dome that displayed my father's pocket watch. Not that it was going to tell me the time. The old watch had stopped running after Dad died.

Dad was a fireman for the Pennsylvania Railroad in the days of steam engines, and he truly worked all the livelong day, as the old song goes. In fact, he was away most of the time, coming back for a few days once a month to collect his paycheck. There was an uneasiness between us when he was home since we talked together so seldom. I never found words to tell him I loved him, or that I was proud of him and his work on the railroad. I sat quietly, just enjoying his company, the ticking of his watch sometimes the only sound in the room.

The watch was a Hamilton, very popular with railroaders. It slipped easily in the small watch pocket that trousers had in those days. Sometimes I wished Dad could slip *me* in his pocket and take me with him on his journeys.

My desk lamp illuminated the dome, and the watch's stainless steel case shone inside. There was a small chip on the edge of its ceramic face, broken off once when it fell to the floor. Still, it had kept running. "A guardian angel looks after this watch," Dad explained.

I knew better. Dad spent an awful amount of time looking after it himself, winding it twice a day, an elaborate process that he allowed me to witness. It was like time stopped for a while. If the hour needed to be reset for some reason, my dad would put the palm of his hand over the crystal faceplate and unscrew it from its case. At the two o'clock position on the edge of the ceramic face was a small lever that had to be pulled up. Once done, he set the correct time by turning the stem. When the lever was down and covered, he could wind the watch.

Dad retired in the 1960s. He became ill soon after and was hospitalized. I visited every day. We were mostly quiet, as always. He kept his faithful timepiece on the nightstand, but it didn't run well anymore. Dad was too weak to take care of it. On the day he died I picked it up. It was no longer ticking. That seemed right somehow. Later I bought the glass dome to display it. I never took the watch to a jeweler. I figured I wouldn't know how to maintain it anyway.

That night sitting at my desk I felt sorry I had never told Dad how I felt. "Why, God? Why didn't I find a way to tell him?" I dropped my head into my hands.

Something startled me. I heard a ticking sound and looked up. It came from my dad's watch. Impossible. I slid the dome closer to the desk lamp. The second hand moved. The watch was running again. Almost as if Dad had heard my thoughts. As if he had heard my thoughts even when I was a boy and knew I loved him. Perhaps a guardian angel did look after Dad's watch and after me.

Out of the Woods

VIRGINIA SCHOENTHALER

It was 2:45 AM according to the clock radio on my night table. I strained my ears for the sound of my son David's car pulling up to the house but heard nothing. *Will this be the night he doesn't make it home at all?*

Of my five children, David had always attracted the most trouble. At two he pulled a dresser over on himself trying to climb it. At six he barely missed being hit by a car while he was riding his bike. "His guardian angel sure gets a workout," my husband, Jeff, and I used to say.

David was nineteen now, and finding more trouble than even his guardian angel could handle. He went around with a bad crowd whose main source of fun was drinking and doing drugs, and David was all too happy to join them. It looked like David's guardian angel had given up on guiding him. *So have I,* I thought, staring up at the ceiling.

Jeff and I had tried everything to get David to turn his life around. Ultimatums, punishments, pleading. David had promised us a dozen times to change his life. "I've really learned my lesson," he'd said six months before. That was after spending a night in jail. He'd been drinking and a policeman found him sleeping it off in his car by the side of the road. He'd charged David with intent to drive under the influence of alcohol. "I see where my life is heading," David told us when we got him home. "No more drugs and no more drinking from now on."

But the next night he went out to meet his friends again. "I'm not going to do anything," he assured us as he pulled on his coat. "I'm just going to hang out. If anybody offers me drugs, I'll just say no."

I wasn't surprised when he came home high again the next morning. David couldn't even admit he had a problem, much less ask for the help he needed to fix it. The words came easily enough, but he wasn't ready to make the kind of changes in his life necessary to give up drugs. For the kind of friends he had now, getting together was just an excuse to get high, and I no longer believed David's promises about a new start. *Lord, David doesn't want my help—or yours. But could you keep his guardian angel close?*

I heard a car outside and sat up in bed. The front door opened and David's footsteps sounded on the stairs outside my bedroom. *Thank you, God, for bringing him home safe one more night!* I pulled on my robe and went to David's room.

"Are you all right?" I asked from the doorway. "It's very late."

David blinked up at me. There was something different about him, but I couldn't put my finger on what it was. *It must be the drugs,* I thought.

"Mom," David said. "An angel drove me home from the party tonight. I swear."

"An angel?" I said. *Yes, definitely drugs.* I was familiar with their effects by now.

"I went to a party out in the woods," David said. "I was high. I started to hallucinate. I thought there were spiders crawling all over my skin."

I shuddered.

"I knew I had to get out of there, but I wasn't fit to drive. My car was parked on the street. Remember how you and Dad used to say I had a guardian angel? I asked God to send him to help me get home." He frowned, as if he were trying to remember what happened. "I must have tried to drive, but it wasn't me at the wheel, Mom. I swear I was in the passenger seat. An angel was behind the wheel!"

I walked into the room and sat down next to him. He was my son, and I loved him no matter what. Even if I hated seeing him like this. "It's okay now. You're home. You're safe."

"The next thing I knew we were parked in front of the house. Mom, God sent me an angel. I'm done messing up. I'm going to change."

"Okay," I said, but how many times had I heard this same speech from David? He would promise to try harder to stay away from drugs and alcohol, but he wouldn't really make a change. "Get some sleep now."

The next day I told Jeff about David's angel story. "He must have still been halluci-nating," I said. David's angel was no more real than his promises. It was all just a fantasy brought on by the drugs. "I'm just glad he didn't get hurt. Or hurt anyone else."

The phone rang and my daughter answered it. "David," she called. "It's your friend on the phone!"

David came into the kitchen. He looked at the phone and shook his head. "Tell him I can't talk to him," he said.

Jeff and I looked at each other in surprise. David never refused friends' calls.

"I can't be with those guys anymore," David said. "If I hang with them I'll just do what I always do." He sat down at the table between his dad and me. "I meant what I said last night," he said. "I really want to change. But I don't think I can do it alone. I need help."

I grabbed David's hand tightly in my own. "David, we want to help you. If only you would really let us."

That night David stayed at home. And the next night. And the rest of the week. Every evening I expected to see him pulling on his jacket to meet his friends, but he continued to refuse their phone calls. *Don't let yourself believe it,* I thought as I went to bed one night, grateful that David was in his own room. *Sooner or later he'll go back to his old ways. He always does.*

Months went by and David stayed away from drugs. I knew that for sure, because he never left the house without one of us with him. "Just in case I'm tempted to get in touch with my friends," he'd explained. He even agreed to attend family counseling sessions and talk about his struggle to our pastor.

"Did David tell you about the angel?" I asked the pastor one Sunday.

"Yes, he insists he was driven home that night. He wasn't behind the wheel."

"He was hallucinating from the drugs," I said. "He doesn't remember driving himself home."

"I don't think it matters if it's true or not," the pastor said. "David draws a lot of strength to fight his addiction from thinking God sent him an angel. Who are we to tell him it didn't happen?"

A few weeks later I was at the supermarket picking up things for dinner. Just knowing David would be joining the family around the table made my shopping more enjoyable. *I should enjoy it while it lasts,* I thought as I got up to the cash register. The man behind me in line helped me unload my cart onto the conveyer belt. "David seems to be doing a lot better," the man said.

"Oh, do you know my son?"

"I live in town," the man said. "One night several months ago my car broke down up there in the woods. I couldn't get any phone reception. I asked God to send an angel to help me and began walking. About five minutes later David crashed out of the trees. I recognized him, although he was very distraught. He was yelling about spiders crawling all over him. He handed me his keys and begged me to drive him home. To tell the truth I was a little afraid of him in that state," the man said, "but I knew if it were my son I'd want him home safe."

I stared at him. "You drove David home?"

"Yup. I watched him get inside safely and used my cell to get a ride home myself. David sure wasn't the angel I expected that night, but he was a lifesaver. My wife and I have been praying for him ever since."

So David's angel was real, all this time, I thought as I drove home from the store. He wasn't a hallucination or one of David's stories. God had answered David's prayer; why couldn't he have answered my own? I believed in David's angel. I believed God was helping him. And now, finally, I believed David had left drugs behind him forever.

On Call

SANDRA UZA PECHTOLD

*M*om was dying. We were all around her—my husband, Bob, and I, my dad, my three kids, my sister and her family. Mom lay in a nursing-home bed, unable to breathe on her own. I sat in a chair, holding her hand. The call had come that morning: "This could be the final forty-eight hours. You should probably come in." We had all made the forty-five-minute drive under a slate-gray sky. A snowstorm was brewing—maybe even a blizzard, the weather report said. Mom lay still, her beautiful chestnut eyes closed by the effects of strong pain medication. In the corner of her room stood a small tree decked with ornaments. It was the day after Christmas.

I looked at Bob. "I can't believe it. In all the rush I forgot—Mom needs a priest to perform last rites." Bob's eyes widened. He glanced out the window.

"Oh my gosh," he said "You're right. I should have thought of it too."

A few snowflakes blew against the glass. Everyone looked at me. A long, paralyzed moment passed.

"I know!" I exclaimed, gently releasing Mom's hand. "I'll look in the phone book." I walked down the hall to the nurse's station and returned with a heavy Yellow Pages.

"Let's see, Churches, Catholic." The clouds outside darkened. My eyes strained in the light from Mom's bedside lamp. I looked for her and Dad's home parish. But it was an hour away at least—too far in this weather.

"Wait. Here's one," I said. "More local." I dialed the phone by Mom's bed.

"Thank you for calling the parish house. We are closed for the holidays. Please leave a message and we will get back to you when we return."

I found another parish, but I heard the same message.

There were many parishes in the phone book. I called most of them. At each, the same message. By the time I reached the end of the list, it was five o'clock. The window was a dark rectangle, lined at the bottom with a layer of snow. Bob shifted uncomfortably.

"Sandra, I think we need to make a decision. The snow's pretty thick out there. We either stay the night or head home."

I looked at Dad, his face strained. I'd never seen him so exhausted. "Okay," I said. "I'll go take this phone book back."

In the hall I ran into Mom's night nurse.

"Your mother appears to be hanging on," she said. "I think if you wanted to go, you could, and come back tomorrow. She'll make it through the night."

Tomorrow! I thought. *Maybe a church will be open by then. But what about the blizzard? Oh, Lord, what can I do?*

"Thank you," I said and walked to the nurse's station. A woman I didn't recognize sat behind the desk. Cindy, her name tag read. "I borrowed this phone book a little while ago. I just wanted to give it back."

The woman took the book from my hands and smiled. "You look troubled," she said. "Can I help with something?"

I slumped against the counter. "I've been trying to find a priest for my mom. She's—well, this could be her last night. But all the churches are closed for the holidays. Not to mention this snow . . ." I trailed off.

Cindy's smile broadened. "Don't worry," she said. "Why don't you go back and sit with your mom? I'll look for a priest. When I find one I'll let you know."

"Would you?" I said. "Thank you so much. I've already called most of the churches in the book. Oh, but I do hope you find one."

"I'm sure I will."

I returned to the room. Everyone was standing. I told them what the nurse had said. And about Cindy.

"You all should probably go on home," I said. "But I think I'll stay here in case Cindy finds someone."

Bob nodded and bent to kiss Mom's cheek. Everyone else did the same and then shuffled into the hall. My son Bobby, who was home from college, offered to stay behind to keep me company.

"Mom will like that," I said. We sat down, and I held her hand again. I thought about her happy, ordinary life. Dad had served in the Navy in World War II and then worked as a machinist in the same shop for thirty-five years until he retired. Mom worked part-time for a while and then volunteered, driving people to the polls on election day. She loved her family—her husband, her kids, her grandkids. I remembered her and Dad, on their forty-eighth wedding anniversary, driving to a Chicago polka-dancing club—their favorite pastime.

"Cindy's looking for a priest for you," I said, squeezing her hand. I thought I felt her squeeze back.

A voice sounded at the door. "I found someone," said Cindy. "Didn't I tell you I would? He will be here to see your mom at nine o'clock."

"Really? How? Oh, thank you!"

"It was no problem," said Cindy. "So don't you worry about a thing. His name is Father Bill."

"Father Bill," I repeated. "Thank you so much, Cindy." She waved and left us alone.

At nine o'clock a priest walked through the door. "I'm Father Bill. How is everyone holding up?"

Bobby and I stood. "Oh, Father, thank you," I said, my voice sounding shaky with relief. Father Bill asked us a few questions and discovered that Bobby had been an altar boy.

"You can help me," he said. Together they made the preparations, and Father Bill anointed Mom and administered communion. At the sound of his voice and his calm, assured movements, a feeling of peace settled over the room. When Father Bill was finished, Mom's breathing was deep and even.

"How did Cindy ever find you on a night like this?" I asked him.

"It's funny," he said. "Ordinarily I wouldn't have been at the church this time of year. I would have been with my family. But this is actually my last day here. I've been called to another parish, in Wisconsin, and I was doing some packing when the phone rang. The snow was pretty heavy, but I promised the woman on the phone I would do everything I could to make it to the hospital. You see, the first priestly act I ever performed in this parish was right here at this nursing home, administering last rites to someone like your mom. So this place is very special to me."

Bobby and I were quiet as Father Bill stood to go. "I can't thank you enough," I said. "It feels like a Christmas miracle."

"Think nothing of it," he said. "It's my job." And he walked out the door.

Mom died peacefully the next day. The first thing I did after the funeral was call the nursing home to thank Cindy for finding Father Bill. The woman at the desk asked me if I might be mistaken about the name of the person who made all the difference for us. "You see," she said, "nobody named Cindy works here. Are you absolutely sure the name tag read Cindy?"

I was sure it did. I was sure about something else too. When everything seemed lost, in the snowstorm, in that dim nursing-home room, God was with us. He knew what we needed. And he sent us an angel to find it.

Marathon Man

CLIFTON C. CARTWRIGHT

People around town call me the Running Doctor. Not because I'm on the go, though my family practice clinic keeps me busy. They mean they've seen me out on the road or in the park or on the college boulevard training for the marathons I compete in all over the country—283 so far in forty-seven states. I started running back when I was a resident to keep my weight down, but it turned out I loved it. There's just something about the way I feel when I'm running that melts away stress.

Well, most of it, anyway. A few years ago I was lining up to begin the Smoky Mountain Marathon in Tennessee. Normally my mind would be on the 26.2 miles ahead of me, but when the starting gun fired all I could think about was my sixteen-year-old son, Wesley. I'd always heard the teenage years were rough on parents, but now I was getting to witness it firsthand.

Wesley wasn't in any real trouble; we simply had silly disagreements about nothing. Talking used to be so easy for us. Now we just could not communicate. Our problem seemed to come out of nowhere.

I took a certain amount of pride in being a good dad, but now I was at a loss as to what I was doing wrong or how I could make things better between us.

I kept up a steady pace on the road. *Do other fathers feel this frustrated in their relationships with their teenagers?* I wondered. *I wish I knew.* I needed this marathon run to get my mind off things.

I rounded a curve coming up on mile three and found myself running beside a man about my age. We nodded to each other. "Where are you from?" I asked.

"Memphis."

My new friend and I seemed to be running at the same pace. A little companionship during a long run was a good thing. My new running buddy's name was Tom. Turned out Tom had a sixteen-year-old daughter. "She's great," Tom said. "Though I don't know how she feels about me these days. It seems like I never say the right thing. No matter how hard I try."

I told him about Wes. "Believe me, I know how that feels," I said. "If I give advice, I'm being pushy. If I give Wes his space, I don't care enough. I don't get it. What am I doing wrong?"

Tom said he had the same dilemma with his daughter. We traded stories, and we even laughed over the similarities in our predicaments. Tom didn't have any real solutions, but knowing someone else was having almost the exact same teen problems made me feel somewhat relieved. "Maybe we're not doing anything wrong," said Tom. "Maybe it's just a growing process—for all of us!"

"You're right," I said at the marker for mile twenty-two. "Wesley's a good kid. I'll probably look back on all this one day and laugh with him about it," I said. "Just like you and your daughter."

"Yeah," Tom said. He dropped a foot or two behind me. "Maybe the key is to remember how much we have to be grateful for in our kids, even when it's hard." He dropped back a little farther. "See you at the finish line!" he called.

"Sure thing!" I waved back and picked up my speed, leaving Tom behind. Once more the rhythm of my feet on the pavement drove any lingering worries from my mind. Running the final four miles I felt lighter, like a weight had been lifted off my shoulders. By the time I reached the finish line I was more than ready to go back to my life as a doctor and a father.

My wife, Carolyn, waited at the end of the marathon. I hugged her, sweaty as I was. She was ready to go home. "Mind if we wait here a couple of minutes?" I asked her. "I want to say good-bye to my running buddy. He helped me more than he could know just by being there."

Carolyn was happy to wait. But the minutes went by without any sign of him. "He shouldn't have fallen so far behind me," I said as we watched yet another runner finish. "Even if he walked the last four miles after we split up. I'm going to check it out."

I walked back onto the course about a mile. A race official was positioned at an intersection. "There's nobody in trouble, is there?" I asked him. "Nobody injured or sick or anything? I'm looking for a friend."

"No one's had trouble, as far as I know," the official said. He checked his walkie-talkie to be sure. "All the racers are fine," he said. "No dropouts."

I hung around for another ten minutes or so before returning to Carolyn at the finish line. *Where could he have gone?* "Maybe Tom dropped out and they just didn't know it," said Carolyn. "There's a lot of people to keep track of."

"Could be," I said. "When I get home I'll check for sure."

The marathon had a website where participants could see their times and results. Every runner was there. I found my own name with my finish time listed. Then I checked for Tom's. "That's odd," I said. "He's not listed at all. According to the records there was no Tom from Memphis, Tennessee, even registered." I turned to Carolyn in confusion. "So who was I running with today?"

I never did find out. Wesley's done a lot more growing up since then. He is a fine young man who knows what he wants to do with his life. We both made it through his adolescence in one piece. Today our relationship is stronger than ever. Maybe Tom wasn't there for the race at all that day. Maybe he was there because I needed him even more than a marathon run.

6

BOLSTERING COURAGE

An angelic command is repeated throughout the Scriptures: "Fear not"—at least that's how it's translated in the King James Version and quoted by Charlie Brown when he's retelling the Christmas story. My young friends seem to resonate with a more contemporary phrasing: "Do not be afraid." The stories in this section relay that message: As angels soothe fears, they complementarily bolster courage—for a mission worker in a Mexican prison, for a high school outsider, for a worried military wife.

My prayer is that these stories will embolden you to step out in faith, as confident as the psalmist: "My heart shall not fear" (Psalm 27:3 RSV).

Traveling Companions

BARBARA J. SHOEMAKER

My husband, Don, retired ten years ago. Soon after, we bought a three-quarter-ton Chevy Silverado and a fully equipped travel trailer, and set off in search of adventure. Our eventual goal was to visit all forty-eight continental states and Canada. We saw New England and New Mexico, and everything in between. One night, deep in Wisconsin wilderness, I marveled at how safe we always felt, no matter how far from home we roamed. "God's angels are with us," I said, and Don nodded, knowing I was right.

Once in Colorado, Don wanted to ride a nineteenth-century train between Durango and Silverton in the Rocky Mountains. I'm scared of heights. "Okay, I'll go," I finally agreed, "but only if our angels come along." I could see nothing below us for thousands of feet, and the track was so narrow the train hung over on both sides. Wonder of wonders, the train ride was thrilling. Those angels were there, all right.

Last summer Don and I had planned a ten thousand-mile journey to the Northwest. We'd covered all but six states and western Canada, and this trip would have been the fulfillment of our dream. Then we had to cancel it. I'd had problems with my right hip for a few years, but so far I had coped. In a very short time, though, the pain grew so bad I couldn't walk. The words "hip replacement surgery" became part of my everyday vocabulary, and fear overtook me.

Not that doctors and hospitals were new to me. I'd lived with diabetes and an irregular heartbeat for years, and I'd also had a couple of strokes. None of this made me a good candidate for surgery. I was afraid. This was something unknown, a journey I'd never taken. Then I remembered the train ride in the mountains of Colorado. I was scared then too, I reminded myself. I had to trust that God would keep me in the company of angels.

"Give Mom a big kiss," Don said when our children came to visit me in the hospital on the morning of my surgery. Some of my good friends stopped by too. Don sat next to my bed, holding my hand. I tried to be cheerful, but it felt like they were all there to say good-bye. In my mind I repeated my favorite psalm over and over again: "He shall give his angels charge over thee . . . " But nothing brought me comfort as the nurse wheeled me to the operating room. Not my friends, my family, not even my prayers.

The gurney stopped outside double doors. Two nurses helped me climb onto the surgical table. As they moved the gurney out of the way, I mouthed a desperate plea: *Lord, I can't make this journey alone!* Then the doors opened with a *whoosh*. Rows of angels stood tall, holy, filling the room. One hovered above the place where the surgical table would be anchored. This was not an unknown place after all. Angels were with me, just as I'd always believed them to be. But now God had let me see them.

Today Don and I are planning short stays in some of the places we've enjoyed before. My recovery has postponed our dream trip till next year. But wherever we go is an adventure; it's a good thing angels come along for the ride.

Gabriel

STEPHEN MUFF

*S*enior year in high school made me ask myself some questions. What did the future hold for me? What kind of work would I do? Where did I belong? One place I never imagined I'd have anything to do with was a Tijuana prison. But there I was, waiting for permission to pass through the gates to where the prisoners were.

Our youth group was in Mexico on a mission trip. We'd been working with kids mostly, hanging out with them, taking them to church. They were so open and friendly. Even the youngest ones tried their best to make us feel at home. They spoke a different language, but underneath they weren't so different from us.

We also did what we could for the community at large. One day I asked our group leader Richard about his work with inmates at the local prison. "I guess it couldn't be more different than my experience with the kids, right?"

Richard surprised me. "Why don't you come and see for yourself? God is among those men as much as he is among the kids." I shrugged. Maybe I'd learn something.

Richard and I rode a clunky bus to the prison and we stepped up to the security gate. A man in a sombrero and a thick moustache typed out a form on an ancient typewriter and then stamped us as visitors. I frowned at the ink on my hand: A purple unicorn? Was I seeing that right?

"Guess they use whatever stamp is available," said Richard. "This isn't like an American prison."

It sure wasn't. There were no bars, cells or chains—and no guards either, once you got inside the walls. It was almost like a village unto itself. Almost. I wouldn't forget for one second that the men around me were criminals.

Richard led me over to the basketball court where men were shooting hoops. We sat on a bench, and he pointed out what was what. There were a couple of makeshift stores and a restaurant, all run by inmates. A line of men waited at a stand for soup. But there was nothing welcoming about this place. It just felt dangerous. Richard got involved in a conversation with one of the inmates. I wondered how they could have anything at all in common. *I can't do anything for these people. And who knows what they might do to me?*

A tall man in a white undershirt and jeans sat down next to me on the bench. "My name is Guillermo," he said. "Some call me Gabriel." He gestured to the man about to take a shot on the court. "See that man there? He's in for murder."

"Oh!" I said. *Great.* "And what about you? Why, uh, why are you in here?"

"Same as you," he said, flashing me a smile. "To spread a message. Everyone deserves to hear it, don't you agree?"

A cheer went up as the man on the court made his shot. When I turned back to Gabriel he was gone. But so quickly?

Richard finished his conversation, and I followed him farther into the prison where children were running around, playing. *Wait—children? In prison?*

"A lot of families come to visit relatives and wind up staying," he said. "Some of their fathers are awaiting trial, some have already been convicted. They are family no matter what."

On a wooden post near some kids playing tag hung a painting of Jesus. It looked out of place, just like the children and families inside these walls. "It's nice, yes?" said Gabriel, suddenly beside me, admiring the painting as if there was nothing strange about it being here. And as if his sudden appearances were nothing out of the ordinary! Still, his presence put me at ease. "You're not a prisoner here, are you?"

Gabriel looked as if he didn't understand the question. "I come here when I'm sent and leave when I'm told to go."

"Oh," I said, supposing he had his reasons for not giving me a straight answer.

Richard moved on. I turned to ask Gabriel if he wanted to walk with us, but he'd disappeared again. "Did you see the guy I was just talking to?" I asked Richard. "Where could he have gone?"

"It's easy to lose sight of people, it's so crowded," he said.

"But I didn't lose sight of him," I said. "He disappeared!" An inmate walked by me. Maybe he knew Gabriel. I got up my courage and tapped him on the shoulder. "Do you know Guillermo?"

"Tall, lanky guy? Moustache?"

"You know him?"

"You must mean Gabriel. No one seems to know for sure where he comes from. He's kind of a mystery to me, but he's a good man. He looks out for us, you know?" He scratched his chin thoughtfully. "Weird, though, how you never see him walk away."

"He just disappears!" I said. "I thought I was going crazy!" There was at least one thing I had in common with an inmate. Neither of us knew what to make of Gabriel. *Maybe I'm not all that different from the people in here.*

"We've got one more place to visit," said Richard. "The high security section, where the violent criminals live. Be careful and stay close."

A guide led the way through a corridor lined with barred cells. I followed Richard closely. A hand rested on my shoulder, warm and reassuring. I knew at once who it was. "Gabriel!"

"Don't worry," he said. "I'm always looking out for you."

He took his hand off my shoulder. An inmate walked toward us from the other end of the corridor. "You got any money?" he asked. I looked straight ahead, trying not to catch his eye. "Come on, you've got money," he repeated, getting angrier. "Give me some money."

Gabriel walked up behind the man. *Wait, he was behind me a second ago,* I thought. *How did he get past me to the other end of the corridor?*

"These people are under my watch," Gabriel told the guy harassing us. "You will leave them alone."

The man moved off without a word. I tapped Richard to show him who Gabriel was, but when I pointed down the corridor, he was gone.

"He must have gotten lost in the crowd again," Richard said.

I was beginning to suspect who—or what—Gabriel was and what he was doing in that prison. God had sent him, just like he'd sent me and Richard. God was watching over this place and everyone in it. He belonged here as much as he did among the village children. That was Gabriel's message for me.

Stranger on the Plateau

SYLVIA ZITTING

Bang! The door slamming jolted me awake. The sky outside my bedroom window was pitch-black. It wasn't anywhere near morning. Whatever time it was, my father was awake and furious.

"Those no-good . . . They're gone!" he said and then yelled, "Everybody up!"

I scrambled out of bed and followed my older sister Geraldine into the kitchen where my parents were. "The field hands have deserted us!" Dad said. "Snuck off in the middle of the night!"

Why would they do that? I thought sleepily. Then I remembered. The afternoon before I'd been tucked up in the hayloft and heard Dad fight with Allen and Jake by the corral. Dad wanted them to drive his herd of horses up Mount Home in the Unitas, across the wide plateau called the Blue Bench, and then back down the other side where our new farm was waiting for us.

"You're crazy!" Allen had said. "You want us to drive one hundred and twenty-five horses up a mountain pass for twenty miles, and another fifty across that God-forsaken Blue Bench all in one day? It's impossible. You've got to truck 'em to your new place!"

"There's no money for trucking," Dad said. "You get your gear together. You're leaving at four o'clock tomorrow morning, so you'd better be ready. It's the only way to get those horses out of these here hills before it snows."

During dinner both Allen and Jake were silent. A terrible silence, louder than any angry words.

They sure were dead set against crossing that Blue Bench, I thought now, standing in the dark kitchen in the middle of the night.

"We've got to move to our new place today, horses and all," Dad told me and Geraldine, his voice going gentle. "Your mom can't drive the truck or those horses. She and I will take your little brothers in the truck with our things. Geraldine, you and Sylvia will have to drive the horses up Mount Home and across the Blue Bench. Nobody's better with horses than you two. You're better than those field hands, even. Just move west to east. I'll meet you on the other side."

Life on a farm wasn't like life in the city, especially back then. Us kids were used to hard work and I was at home on a horse. But if two grown men didn't want to do it, how could Dad give such a job to Geraldine, at seventeen, and me, only twelve? Get all those horses up a mountain, across fifty miles of dirt, sagebrush and sky in all directions? What if we needed help up there? *Don't you care what happens to us?* I wanted to ask, but nobody said no to Dad. And for good reason. He usually knew what he was doing.

Geraldine and I saddled up. I rode Hytone, my favorite, a big, beautiful palomino. As the sun rose so did my spirits. We followed a mountain road lined with quaking asps, pine trees and lots of grass for the horses to graze on. Trees canopied the road. Glimmers of sunlight danced through the dewy leaves. Geraldine and I giggled, sang songs and yodeled at the top of our lungs. Two girls were doing what seasoned field hands couldn't!

We watered the horses at a creek; then Geraldine rode out in front to guide them onto the top of the plateau. I followed behind the herd. The Blue Bench was as desolate as I remembered, full of washes and ravines. Seeing it laid out before me I wondered if we'd ever reach Dad on the other side. Maybe those field hands had the right idea by running away. It was just Geraldine and me, abandoned with the herd. "We have to be really careful," Geraldine warned me, "not to lose any of the horses back in those ravines."

The horses' hooves stirred up clouds of dust. We kept them close together. Too much space and some young renegade was sure to break ranks and race off to parts unknown, tail waving straight up in the air. Then we'd have to go racing after him. Looking out over their backs to the north I saw the peaks of the Unitas glistening with summer snow.

We pushed out over the dusty land. There was no yodeling now. I was plain mad. My mouth was parched. My butt ached in the saddle. I squirmed side to side, but it didn't help. My shoulders and neck hurt too. "Are we about there?" I cried out. "How much longer?" No answer. Geraldine couldn't hear me way out in front when I added, "My body feels like dying!" *Nobody would care if I did die up here,* I thought.

We pressed on, hour after hour, until the sun got low and the wind picked up. Heavy black clouds gathered over our heads. Now, as well as being tired, thirsty and mad, I was scared. "Dad'll never find us in a storm," I yelled. "He cares more about his horses than he cares about us!" I laid my head on Hytone's strong neck and bawled.

But my bawling didn't stop the rain pouring down on us a moment later. The horses turned their backs to the storm, dropped their heads and refused to move. *This is as bad as it gets,* I thought. Then it started to hail.

Geraldine rode her horse over to me. She looked as miserable as I felt. "This hail's beating us up!" she yelled over the wind. We huddled close to the horses' warm bodies for shelter. "I guess we know what hell is like, don't we?" Geraldine yelled. We sure did.

We pressed together in the thick black night as the wind battered us. When the storm finally let up a little, Geraldine said, "Let's get on our horses. We must be almost there by this time."

I climbed up on Hytone and tried to urge the horses forward. A flash of lightning showed they were wandering off, hunting for food. "Hey, I'm hungry too, but we've got to get off this God-forsaken Blue Bench!" I yelled as Geraldine and I chased them back into line. I was shivering wet in my clothes. "Dad!" I screamed. "Where are you?" The wind pushed my voice right back in my face. I probably would have cried again if I wasn't so tired.

"I'm going to look for a way off this plateau," said Geraldine.

She disappeared in the darkness, and I felt like the last person in the world I could count on was gone. I was abandoned in this desolate place, lost. Lightning flashed again, showing only the same dirt and sagebrush I'd been staring at all day. "God!" I called out. "I need you now. Please! I'm farm-raised and tough, sure. But I'm still just a kid!"

Another bolt of lightning struck. It illuminated the sky—and something else. The outline of a figure. What was it? A man on a horse? "Dad!" My heart swelled. Courage surged through my body. *Dad's come for us!* I'd never loved my father so much as in that moment. I realized we weren't abandoned. Maybe I was just a kid, but I felt like I could do anything.

"Come on," I yelled to the horses. "We're getting off this plateau now!"

Another flash of lightning showed me our savior again. He was smiling proudly, like he was just as happy to see me as I was to see him. He motioned for me to come his way. Hytone trotted ahead like he was following the signal too, his tired muscles moving fast under my legs, stepping onto a narrow path I would never have found without Dad to guide me.

I met Geraldine at the bottom right beside a road. We'd made it off the Blue Bench, and we hadn't lost one horse. "Which way should we go?" Geraldine said, looking up and down the road.

That was a silly question—we would just follow Dad when he got down. But before I could say anything, a truck pulled up. Down rolled the window and out popped Dad's face.

"You made it!" he said. "Good work! Now just follow me down the road a bit and we'll be home." He started to raise the window and stopped. "I'm really sorry I didn't meet you on the plateau," he said. "I couldn't find a way up there in this storm."

Couldn't find a way up? I thought. *Then who . . . ?*

I twisted round in my saddle and looked back up to the Blue Bench far above my head. Lightning lit the sky. The man on the horse waved down to me, smiling and proud at what we'd done. I still felt him watching over me as I turned to follow Dad home in the truck. Dad had not been able to lead us down the mountain himself, but I was never alone on that plateau. And I would never be abandoned.

One of the Crowd

KYLE WOODARD

Different. That's what I've always been. As far back as kindergarten, the other kids saw I was clumsy and got really distracted sometimes. They didn't want to be friends, so God and I got extra close. One night in my room, when I was five years old, he even spoke to me. "Kyle," he said, "this is God. You're going to have a baby sister." Sure enough, a few days later Mom found out she was pregnant. My new sister, Libby, never shied away from me or laughed when I fell down. I wished the other kids could see me the way she did. *God,* I wondered, *what makes me different?*

I was about to start first grade when my doctor discovered I had a massive brain tumor. Mom did her best to help me understand my condition. "You are going to need an operation, Kyle," she said.

"Will I die?"

Tears sprang to Mom's eyes. "We'll be praying hard that doesn't happen, honey. But remember, God is waiting for all of us in heaven." She hugged me tight. I'd read about heaven in the Bible, but I wasn't sure I wanted to go there. What if heaven was just like school? What if nobody wanted to be my friend there either?

A few months after my first tumor was removed, doctors discovered another tumor, another one that required surgery. During this second operation I felt myself lifting out of my body. Floating in the air, I watched the doctors operating, passing instruments and checking machines. Then a bright white light appeared. I moved toward it down a long tunnel. At the end was Jesus. He took me by the hand and walked me down a red carpet. Rows of angels stood on either side, their large wings arched high above their heads, waving to me like I was their friend. "Welcome, Kyle!" they said. I was so excited I jumped and ran—two things I hadn't been able to do in a long, long time. Then I saw my Uncle Sterling, who had died several years before. "I don't ever want to leave," I told him. I raced into his arms. Uncle Sterling held me close and said gently, "You'll have to go back, Kyle. It's not your time."

Go back? I thought. Now that I knew how it felt to be completely accepted? "No way!" I shouted. "It's true, Kyle," a man answered. His voice sounded familiar. I'd heard it before . . . that night in my room when I was five. "I have a special plan for you," he said.

I tried to remember those words when I went back to school, which was worse than ever. Steroids I took to reduce post-op swelling had made me put on forty pounds, and I had to wear a helmet to protect my skull. My brain tumor never went away completely, and doctors believed I didn't have long to live. My eyesight got so bad I had to walk with a cane. I was in and out of school—and the hospital. By the time I was in fifth grade I'd lost many good friends, all with terminal diseases like me. But at school I was the boy with the brain tumor. The boy with the cane. The boy who was different.

That Christmas, my family, whose extra money all went toward my treatment, was "adopted" by the students of Shadle Park High School. We got a care package with a holiday dinner, toys for Libby and a Shadle Park sweatshirt for me. I took it straight up to my room to try on. Pulling it over my head, I pictured myself as a teenager at Shadle Park High walking proudly down the hall in a sweatshirt like this. So what if my dream seemed impossible? Doctors thought it was impossible I'd live this long. And God said he had a plan for me. Was it too much to ask that it include Shadle Park High? Against all odds, I walked through the doors of Shadle Park High as a freshman four years later. Sure, I wasn't exactly one of the crowd, but I wasn't going to let that stop me now. I attended football games, pep rallies and school dances, where I stood to the side, tapping my cane to the music, occasionally finding a girl willing to dance with me.

Sophomore year I started helping out with the adopt-a-family program that had provided me with the Shadle Park High sweatshirt. Still, there were times I envied my "normal" classmates. *Just once I want to be Kyle, instead of "the guy who's dying,"* I thought one afternoon as I sat in the library. Someone tapped me on the shoulder. It was Principal Arndt. "Kyle," he said, "we're having an assembly on Friday. Would you give a talk on the adopt-a-family program?"

Normally I might have been reluctant to get up in front of the whole school, but the adopt-a-family program was important to me. Besides, hadn't God said he had a plan for me? Maybe this was it. "Okay," I said. "I'll do it."

The day of the assembly I got up onstage in the auditorium. "Coming to school here was a dream of mine," I began. I told the kids about how left out I'd felt in grade school. Then I talked about the sweatshirt and my fantasy of how cool I'd be once I was a student at Shadle Park High. They laughed, but I could tell they were laughing because it was a fantasy they'd all entertained. "That simple sweatshirt gave me hope of belonging when I was sure I'd never be accepted anywhere," I concluded. "And every kid should have a chance to feel like that. Even those of us who aren't the most popular."

Junior year, my only memory of being completely accepted was still that moment in heaven. Lying awake after a particularly disastrous dance, I made a bold request: *I know you have a plan for me, God. But just once I'd like to feel that good again here, on earth.* Then I went to sleep and let God think it over.

A few weeks later we filed into the auditorium for an assembly. When we were all settled, the student body president, Tom Friedlander, got up to hand out varsity letters to those lucky athletes who'd qualified for them. "Letters are awarded to players who have proved most valuable to the team," Tom explained. I wondered which of my classmates were about to get the green *S* that was like a big hug from the whole entire school. "Letters are given for football, basketball, baseball and track," Tom went on, building the suspense. "This year, the Student Association has added a new category, courage. And—by unanimous vote—the first to receive a letter in courage is Kyle Woodard."

Did he just say I lettered? The kids sitting behind me gave me a gentle push forward. As I walked up to the front of the auditorium with my cane, I heard the rumble of 1,700 students rising to their feet, cheering. I didn't need twenty-twenty vision to know they had the same expressions on their faces as the angels that had rolled out the red carpet for me in heaven. *You're one of us,* the kids were telling me. *Welcome, Kyle.*

You couldn't peel that letterman jacket from my back. When people passed me in the hall, I smiled, knowing they were looking at my name and the green S stitched beside it. "That stuff you said at assembly really got me thinking," one girl said. "Remember how you talked about feeling like everybody thinks you're weird? That's just how I feel a lot of the time."

Over and over I heard the same thing. Kids seemed to use congratulating me on the jacket as an excuse to tell me their secrets. Feeling different, which I'd always thought kept me isolated, was the very thing that brought me closer to them. They were experiencing these feelings for the first time, but I was already an expert! Who better to help them than me? Finally I was just one of the crowd. And part of a very special plan.

The Meaning of Good-bye

RACHAEL FABANICH-MCBRIDE

Jack, my young son, held my hand tightly as we walked up to the hospital entrance. "This won't take long at all, sweetie," I said. "The doctor just needs to take a picture of your chest. Then we'll go meet Grandma and Nathan, and you can tell your brother all about it."

Jack never liked going to the doctor, but because of his asthma my husband and I weren't taking any chances. He had quite a wheeze and only a chest X-ray could assure us he didn't have pneumonia.

We pushed through the doors into a long corridor that led to the X-ray rooms. Immediately my mind flew back to my last visit in these very halls, when my father was being treated for gastric cancer. It wasn't yet a month since Dad had died. I gave Jack's hand a squeeze. My son couldn't know it, but today Mommy wanted to be here even less than he did. These hospital walls just reminded me of the good-bye I never wanted to hear.

"This is where they took care of Pap," Jack said, looking around at the sterile hallway.

"Yes, you're right," I said.

"Pap is with Jesus now," Jack said.

"Yes, he is," I said. "That's a wonderful place to be." *Even if I wish he could be with Jack and me. Here. Now.* But that wasn't to be. This good-bye was forever.

In the waiting room, Jack pressed close to me. "There's nothing to be scared of," I assured him. "The doctor is going to take a picture of you with a special camera. You'll have to stand real still like a statue."

"Do I have to smile?" Jack asked, his face drawn with worry. I assured him he didn't have to smile. I didn't think he could have smiled if he tried.

The nurse called our name and I took Jack into the exam room. The friendly technician let me hold his hand as she lowered the camera to his height. "Now, hold very still," she said. "We want to get a good picture of you."

Jack stood in place. "Okay," the technician said. "Ready or not—"

Jack suddenly twisted around to me. "Mommy!" he whispered. "I have to tell you something important."

"Let the lady take your picture and then you can tell me," I said.

Jack shook his head. "No, Mommy! I have to tell you now."

I turned helplessly to the technician. "I'll just be a second," I said and kneeled down to Jack's level. "What is it?"

"Pappy's here," Jack said. "Look." Jack pointed across the room. "He's waving to me. Don't you see him, Mommy? He's waving."

I didn't know what to say. *No, Jack,* I thought. *We had to say good-bye to him. . . .*

But Jack was insistent. "He looks like a bright light. His feet are not even touching the floor!" Jack broke into a grin and waved his hand as hard as he could. "Hi, Pap!" he said. "They're going to take my picture. Now I'm not even scared anymore!"

I couldn't see Jack's vision, but the absolute trust on my son's face was more than enough to make me believe. I waved too. Why not? Dad hadn't gone away forever. Even if I couldn't see him now, I would again someday.

Jack turned back to me. "I can't wait to tell Nathan!" he said.

"Okay," I said to the technician. "I guess he's ready." His confidence high, Jack stood perfectly still for his X-ray. Results showed he did not have pneumonia. Nathan and my mother met us in the hospital lobby. Jack told them all about seeing his Pap. They weren't sure quite what to make of Jack's story. But I did. Jack trusts that Pap is here with us even though he can't see him. I didn't have that trust. Not until that day.

In the Watches of the Night

SUSAN JONES

*M*iddle of the night phone calls were nothing new in our house. My husband, Curt, rolled over to take this one. "Looks like the *Catenary* needs me early," he said after he hung up. "The weather's getting bad and the tide's coming in fast. I'm on watch until morning. We'll be on the river at dawn. I have to get there ASAP. "

I pulled on some clothes and went to bundle up our two children for the car ride. Curt had served in the Coast Guard for years. Fourteen days out of every month he was away from home, patrolling the Delaware River. I should have been used to it by now. But the truth was, every time Curt left home I was afraid. Curt couldn't always tell me about his missions, but I knew they could be dangerous.

Any given night the crew might rescue boaters in trouble, put out a dock fire or chase down criminal activity such as drug traffic. Sometimes Curt couldn't even tell me where he was going because the information was classified. Alone with our two young children, I worried about him each second he was gone, imagining the dangers he could get into.

"Come on, honey," I whispered, wrapping Elizabeth in a blanket. I lifted Daniel out of his crib and carried him downstairs.

It was early spring, but the night was chilly. I buckled Daniel into his car seat. Curt tossed his sea bag inside the trunk.

"It's just a routine patrol," Curt said as we drove to the station in Gloucester City. "Nothing special."

But routine patrols could get un-routine very quickly. Driving Curt to the station wasn't so bad, but I already dreaded the drive home, when I would be all alone with the children and my worries.

We reached the base in Gloucester City and a soldier at the gate waved us through. My fears doubled as we passed through the gate and the USCGC *Catenary* came into view. Curt loved the sixty-five-foot US Coast Guard cutter. She had an excellent commanding officer and an experienced crew. But all I saw when I looked out at the dock was the tug that would take my husband into the unknown, leaving me behind with my fears. "Dear Lord," I whispered as I pulled the car into the lot, "give Curt your protection and me your peace."

A solitary light mounted on a storage shed cast a beam of light on the pier. The *Catenary* was tied to the dock, riding low in the water. As soon as the tide came in, she would set out. Behind the *Cat* was her sister cutter, the *Cleat*. Both ships looked empty.

"The *Cleat*'s just got back from patrol tonight," said Curt. "Her crew's probably all gone home by now, except the watchmen."

I nodded. The whole base looked deserted, though I knew the seven other men in Curt's crew were already on board the *Cat* sleeping, ready to leave early in the morning. Curt's watch would start as soon as he got on board and last until the morning.

Curt leaned over to the kids sleeping in the backseat and kissed them both; then he turned back to me. "Try not to worry while I'm gone," he said, giving me a kiss. "I love you."

I tried to smile, but it was a struggle not to cry when he got out. *If only I could be brave,* I thought as Curt walked round to the trunk to get his sea bag. *If only I could trust Curt will be okay. That we will both be okay.*

Curt slammed the trunk shut, walked to the gangway and down a ramp that led to the floating dock where the *Cat* was anchored. I climbed into the driver's seat and gripped the steering wheel hard, trying to get myself together. My eyes went to the boat again, hoping to see Curt.

That's when I noticed a young woman sitting on the pier, between my car and the edge. *What's she doing here?* She wore jeans and a plaid shirt without a jacket—surprising on a chilly night like this one with the wind blowing off the water. If she felt the cold, she didn't show it. She didn't even seem aware of my car idling not ten feet away from her. She just stared intently out at the *Catenary.* I wondered who she could be.

Her golden blonde hair caught the light from the storage shed and cast a glow around her face. She didn't seem to be looking for anyone. Her face was serene but watchful, as if she had a purpose there, some job she was doing. But what job could she have at this military station at this time of night? Maybe she has a boyfriend or a husband on the boat she's seeing off. It was a comforting thought. I'm not the only one left behind tonight. Looking at this girl sitting calmly on the dock, I felt calmer too.

Curt appeared on the deck of the tug, ready to begin his watch. I waved to him from the car and pointed to the girl who sat between us. Curt gave me a final salute and then disappeared into the ship's cabin.

I pulled the car around to head back to the gate. The woman on the pier never moved or showed she noticed me. Glancing in the rearview mirror, I had the strangest feeling like I was leaving her with Curt. Even stranger, that it seemed right. As I passed by the guard on the way out of the base, my mind was filled not with worries about Curt or fears about the days alone ahead, but with the memory of the girl's calm, watchful face.

Her face stayed with me all through the drive home in the dark, and it was the first thing I thought of when I woke up the next morning. Each day of Curt's tour I expected to be swamped by my fears the way I always had been in the past. But each time I felt overwhelmed taking care of the children alone, or when I thought of Curt patrolling on the river at night, the girl came to my mind, sitting on the dock in her plaid shirt, the light from the storage shed making her glow. It was almost as if she was giving her calm strength to me whenever I thought about her.

Curt was gone for five days. The kids and I drove back to the base to pick him up. We all jumped out of the car to give him a group hug. "It was a good patrol," he said as we drove home. "No trouble at all."

"Same for me," I said, happy at how much I meant it. "But there's one thing I have to ask you. Do you know who that girl was on the dock the night I dropped you off?"

"What girl?" asked Curt.

"The blonde girl in the plaid shirt. She was sitting, watching the boat when I dropped you off. Remember? I pointed her out, but you couldn't have missed her anyway. Was she somebody's girlfriend? Maybe she was there saying good-bye to somebody that night?"

Curt gave me a puzzled look. "All the men in my crew were asleep when I got there. There was no girl on the dock the night you dropped me off. I should know. Remember, I was the one on watch until dawn!"

There was no way Curt could have missed the girl that night, but just to be sure he asked the men. He even asked the guys on the *Cleat* if they knew who she was. But by then I had figured out who the girl was and why Curt hadn't seen her on the dock that night. She was the *Catenary*'s angel, standing guard over "those in peril on the sea" as the old Navy hymn goes. She had always watched over Curt and his men. Only that night she knew I needed to see her. She showed me that angels were watching over all our family, on the sea and on the land.

7

SPEAKING

PROPHETICALLY

To the man or woman who is acquainted with God and who knows
how to pray, there is nothing remarkable in the answers that come.
—E. M. BOUNDS

Some of our stories have shown angels in action, guarding, guiding, watching. But this next band of our procession features stories in which angels speak into the future; and time proves the truth of their messages—delivered in a mother's dream, by a man who knocks at the door, by a grandfather as he dies.

May these stories imprint hope in your heart and reassure you that at all times—now and in the future—a heavenly presence cares for you and answers all your prayers, even before you call.

Sylvester's Prophecy

ROB KRESS

By the time my daughter Katie Lynn was six months old, she had undergone two major operations. Her chest looked like a road map of stitches and scars. Now she faced a third operation for a blood clot that had resulted from her last heart surgery. At 1:30 on a Friday afternoon in 1990, the surgeons at Children's Hospital of Michigan started to operate. She wasn't returned to the cardiac unit until eight thirty that night.

Although the surgery was successful, we didn't know how long it would be before Katie could come home. The next day my wife, daughter and son and I sat by her bed. When visiting time was up, I went to get the car. Carolyn, my wife, wanted to spend a few minutes alone with Katie. Our son and daughter stopped at the cafeteria for a Coke.

As I waited for them in the lobby, I was joined by a man who stepped out from behind a pillar. He wore a workman's blue coveralls and a hat; his hands were stained with grease. "How you doing, Rob?" he asked.

A little startled, I replied, "Good. How are you?" Sometimes people recognized me from my nightly weather report on a local TV station.

"I hear that your daughter is going home tomorrow."

I shrugged and shook my head. "I don't think so. The doctors say she'll be lucky if she can go home in a week."

"Maybe I misunderstood." With that he leaned up against the pillar, smiling kindly. "They call me Sly," he introduced himself, "short for Sylvester."

I nodded; then I looked down at the floor. When I looked up, Sly was gone.

We were on our way home, heading up I-75, when I suddenly turned to Carolyn and declared, "Katie is coming home tomorrow."

She looked at me as if I'd lost my mind. "Rob, that's impossible. Katie won't be home for at least a week." *She's right*, I thought, trying to dismiss the strange idea.

The following morning Carolyn and I were back at Children's Hospital. As we entered the cardiac unit, Katie's nurse stopped us. "I've been trying to reach you with a message," she exclaimed. "Katie can go home."

"What?" Carolyn asked.

"Katie is healed. The doctors are astounded!"

But I was even more astounded. The message had already been delivered.

A Knock at the Door

COLLEEN L. REECE

Bitter cold surrounded the farmhouse. The snow that had pelted the countryside during the day now swirled about with every gust of wind. The porch of the old house lay covered with a thick white carpet, and ice stood solid in the water bucket.

Inside, the youngest child lay sick. The doctor, who had fought his way through the storm earlier, left strict orders: "Keep the baby warm." He measured medicine into a small bottle. "Give him this," he instructed the child's mother. "The fever should run its course in a few days." The doctor then pulled his coat collar high and left, anxious to get his horse and buggy back over the five snow-clogged miles of road that stretched between the isolated farm and town. Soon the route would be impassable.

For the rest of the afternoon, the baby slept. The mother prepared supper while her husband and the boys struggled to the barn to milk and care for the animals.

"Whew!" the father exclaimed when they came back in. "What a howler." He rubbed his icy hands and shook snow from his coat. When his family gathered around the table, the man bowed his head, "Father, we have much to be thankful for. We are grateful for this, thy bounty and thy loving care. Bless us all in Jesus' name and for his sake, amen."

"Amen" echoed around the table, interrupted by the baby's hoarse cry. The woman went to the handmade cradle, picked up her little son and exclaimed, "Why, this child is burning up!"

The eldest son, in his teens, shoved back his chair and stood. "Anything we can do?"

"I don't think so. I'll sponge him off." The mother's hands caressed the fussy child.

"Shall I ride for the doctor?" The eldest son's question brought silence around the table. *On a night like this?*

The woman shook her head. "No. The doctor can't do anything more—even if he could get through."

"Ma's a good nurse," the father reminded them. His simple statement brought reassurance, and the family silently finished their meal. In those days there was little a parent could do besides keeping a child comfortable.

The girls quickly cleared the table and washed the dishes. The fireplace roared; the backlog radiated heat into the big room. The boys sat on the wood floor, each with his own harness-mending job.

The hands of the clock limped around their course. The storm increased. Something made a thump outside. The eldest son raised his head from his work. "What was that? No one in his right mind would be out on such a night." He crossed to the heavy door, swung it wide and let in a wintry blast. A stranger stood on the porch.

"Come in, man, come in." The eldest son motioned the stranger inside and hastily closed out the wind that set the curtains dancing. "What are you doing out in this blizzard? Let me go outside and see to your horse."

"I have no horse." The stranger smiled. "I wondered if I might have something to eat."

"No horse?" The eldest son looked at his father. *What manner of man would be afoot in such weather?*

The woman, still busy with her sick child, admonished, "Don't keep the poor man standing in his wet coat, Pa. Help him out of it. Girls, give our visitor something to eat."

They quickly filled a plate with the remains of supper. Cornbread, still a little warm. Beans. A glass of milk. Pickle relish. "I'm sorry it isn't more," one of the girls said. Her honest eyes looked into his.

"This will be fine." The stranger's gaze rested on her tangled curls and sweet face, and then turned when the baby cried out.

"He's sick," a little one said. "But Ma's a good nurse."

"Don't worry," the stranger said, "he will be fine." Then he began to eat.

The woman looked up, caught by the assurance in his voice. Not wanting to embarrass their guest by watching him eat, the boys continued their harness mending.

"Thank you for the food." The stranger stood. "I'll be going now." Before they could do more than stare, he slipped into his coat and out the door.

"Stop him," the father commanded. "He can stay here overnight. He mustn't go out in this—"

The eldest son ran to the door and flung it open. He stepped to the porch, shivering. "Come back," he shouted into the night. "Come back and stay with us!"

Only the howling wind replied.

He called again. "Mister, we have room for you." When he received no answer, he went back inside and swallowed hard. "He's gone."

"Gone! Where? He will freeze. Go after him, son." The father quickly lighted a lantern and thrust it into his son's hand. The young man gripped the collar of his coat and let the door shut behind him.

"Ma, Pa, come here," he called from outside. His father opened the door and the others crowded behind him. The eldest son held the lantern high. Its light joined the light from the room and illuminated the porch, steps and front yard.

The snow lay unbroken.

There were no footprints on the white expanse.

The family stared at the unblemished drifts, heedless of the blowing snow.

"But he went out this door!" the man protested. "We all saw him. Where did he go?"

Father and sons searched the porch, yard, nearby trees—to find no footprints but their own.

"Ma says come quick!" one of the girls called from the porch. "Hurry!"

Shivering and wet, they rushed back inside. "Is the baby worse?" the man asked.

"No," the woman answered quietly. "The fever is broken. The child is sleeping peacefully. Come and look."

"Praise the Lord!" The man's exclamation shone in the others' faces.

The eldest son turned from the baby to the door. "The stranger said the baby would be fine. But who was he and where did he go, Pa?"

The man started to shake his head and then went to the mantel and took down the big family Bible. His gnarled, work-worn hands turned to a marked passage, and he read from the Book of Hebrews in an unsteady voice, "Be not forgetful to entertain strangers: for thereby some have entertained angels unawares."

The woman asked the question hovering on all their lips. "Do you think the stranger was an angel?"

Her husband closed the Bible. "I don't know. He came to this house. We fed him. He said the child would be fine. I don't know that it was an angel. I do know that a man leaves tracks in the snow."

More than eighty years have passed since the stranger visited the farmhouse of the sick child. Four generations have heard the story and speculated. Because of this story my own life has been influenced, my belief and faith in God strengthened. You see, I know the story to be true. The eldest son was my father.

Mama's Dream

SAMMER ALLAMADANI

Breakfast was my favorite, though Mama made it hard to choose with her delicious cooking for every meal. One morning at home in Damascus before school I sipped Mama's rich tea and devoured her fried eggs, soft cheese and salty olives.

"Sammer, I had such a nice dream," she said. "You were happy and laughing, in a green forest by the sea."

"Yes, Mama," I said. I loved the sea. My best memories were of family visits to the Mediterranean when I was little.

"An angel carried you to this green place," Mama said. "And there were people speaking all the languages of the world."

My mother believed in angels. She often had nice dreams, and some of them had come true. Thanks to the angels, she claimed. But this one was impossible. "There are no forests by the sea in Syria," I said. At sixteen I longed to see the world, but I saw a future for me only in Damascus. Perhaps I would be a teacher like my mother and father. I woke early every morning just to read and study. Education meant everything to me. I'd have to find my adventure in books.

Yet my mother's odd dream stayed in my mind. *An angel to fly me to the seaside,* I thought on the way to school. *That would take a miracle.*

One day after a soccer game I noticed a scrap of paper on the ground. I saw the word "scholarship." I picked up the paper. The United Nations Center in Damascus announced a competition for a two-year, all-expenses-paid scholarship to a college in Italy. Only one high school student in Damascus would be chosen. *Has God given me a miracle?* I thought. My grades were the best in my school. I headed for the UN Center, walking for more than an hour to reach it. "Everyone has applied," the UN clerk said. "It will be tough to win." I told no one about my application, not my family or friends. *I'll tell them after I win.*

Weeks passed and I heard nothing. Finally, I told my parents. "Two hundred students from seventy countries throughout the world," I said. I had given up the dream that I'd be chosen.

"We will go to the UN Center and check," said my father. There we learned my fears were true. Another boy was the winner. I was silent all the way home.

"Life is full of other beautiful things," Mama said. "Come. You will love what your mama cooked."

Not long after, my mother met me at the door when I returned from school. "Someone called," she said. "From the United Nations." The winner had refused at the last moment. I was second on the list. "You won the scholarship from the United World College of the Adriatic!" Mama shouted.

Mama helped me pack. Every night she hid food in my luggage, and every morning I took it out. "Too heavy," I said. But the very last day she managed to hide as much as she liked. Early on an August morning my parents went with me to the airport. "Don't cry, Mama," I said. "Have a good smile. It will make me stronger." But my mother's tears were flowing. I was afraid. I had never been in an airplane. I had never left my country. My language was Arabic. I knew no Italian and very little English. What if I got lost? And in the Rome airport, I did. I missed the connecting flight to Trieste, and slept fitfully in a metal chair all night. I was glad for Mama's food then.

"Welcome to Italy!" said the American who met me at the Trieste airport the next morning. With him was a guy from Denmark and a girl from Spain. I didn't understand a word they said. The ride to the school was a blur. I wished I had a cup of Mama's tea to wake me up. The driver dropped us off at the villa where we'd live. I put my bags down and went for a walk, half asleep. Everything was quiet except for the pounding of my heart. Or was it something else?

I stood still. There, only a few steps ahead, was the Adriatic Sea. I'd heard the waves crashing onto the shore. Could this be possible? I turned to view more of my surroundings. Around me towered the largest forest I could have ever imagined, mountains of green embracing the buildings of the school. My school. This was my dream of adventure and my mother's angel dream come true. A green forest by the sea.

Pop's Prophecies

LORI A. KENNEDY

Grandfather's name was Sebastian, but everyone called him Pop, so I did too. He was central to my early life in Pennsylvania because I spent so much time at my grandparents' home. While Grandma cooked her hearty Italian meals, Pop serenaded me on his mandolin, the one he'd slung over his shoulder when he emigrated from Sicily. He'd light his pipe and let the gray smoke curl above his snow-white hair. A warm smile like that of a man in love spread across his face as he played. His long, slender fingers strummed songs he remembered from his childhood.

Pop had another gift along with his talent for music. Grandma called it prophecy. He accurately predicted the weather, and he saw things in people they couldn't see in themselves. Pop was a quiet observer who gently prodded with suggestions and reassurances. One summer Pop declared that a neighbor's troublesome teenage son would be a doctor someday. "The family couldn't believe it," Grandma told me, "but sure enough the boy became a surgeon."

Before I made any big life decisions, I always talked things over with Pop first. He played his mandolin, asked all the right questions and we came to a solution. His advice never failed me. I often thought his wisdom was inspired by God himself. Maybe angels whispered the messages in his ear.

My marriage (blessed by Pop) took me too far away from Pennsylvania—to California. How I missed Pop's mandolin music and his guidance. I visited only once a year, but we kept in touch with frequent phone calls. One call was particularly bittersweet. "I have good news and not so good news," I said. I was pregnant with my first child. "I can't come home for my annual visit," I said. After two hospital stays my doctor insisted I spend the last trimester in bed. I confided this only to Pop and just said "I'm fine" to everyone else. I knew I could count on Pop to keep whatever I told him to himself.

"I dream about the baby every night," I said. "I wonder if it's a girl or a boy. Then I wonder if I'm eating the right foods and taking the right vitamins. I worry my baby won't be healthy."

Pop said he'd keep me in his prayers as always; then he gave the phone to Grandma to finish the conversation. I could hear him strumming his mandolin softly in the background. I needed Pop more than ever. Only he could ease my worries. He would have the answers to my questions. Our phone calls weren't enough.

One night I was startled awake. I expected to see my husband sitting on the side of the bed, as he often did when my worried dreams about my baby made me restless. But I turned over to find him asleep beside me. When I looked back I thought I saw Pop sitting there with me, big as life. I must be dreaming.

"Pop, what are you doing here?" I asked. He seemed so real.

"I want you to know everything will be fine for you and the baby," he said. "You will have a healthy boy. He will have the gift of music. Like me."

Pop's eyes sparkled, and then he stood up and walked out of the room. I heard the sweet sound of his mandolin playing somewhere in the night.

The music changed to ringing, louder and louder. A hand touched my shoulder. My eyes flew open. "It's the telephone," my husband said. So I had been dreaming about Pop after all.

I reached for the phone on my nightstand. It was Grandma's sister. She spoke softly into the phone like she was shielding the receiver with her hand so no one else could hear. "I have bad news," she said. "Pop passed over in his sleep. Your grandma was afraid to tell you because you're so close to having the baby, but I knew you'd want to know."

Five days later I gave birth to a healthy baby boy. We christened him with the middle name of Sebastian in memory of my grandfather. His love of music was evident at an early age. He happily strummed Pop's mandolin and taught himself to play several instruments, including the guitar. As I watch his long, slender fingers glide across the strings, I remember my dream, unlike any dream I've ever had. The angels who whispered prophecies to Pop brought his final message to me.

The Angel Came on Wednesday

ANN CANNADY

*U*ntil that incredible morning, I thought that angels were something you saw on Christmas cards or read about in the Bible. I never conceived of them as beings who could step into our lives.

Seventeen years ago my life was in terrible turmoil. At forty-four, I had recently been diagnosed with uterine cancer. I agonized over the possibility that I might leave my four children motherless. My husband, Gary, a strapping former Air Force master sergeant, was devastated. He had lost his first wife to the same type of cancer. He took me in his arms and with tears streaming down his face said, "I can't bear the thought of losing you."

My doctor scheduled a radical hysterectomy for later in the month at Cape Fear Valley Hospital. Meanwhile, Gary and I did the only thing we could—we prayed. Every day we knelt together and asked God to heal me, to give us time to raise our children. Friends and fellow members of the Haymount United Methodist Church prayed for me as well. We had everyone we knew praying. But as the surgery date loomed, I felt my faith begin to waver. What lay ahead seemed so frightening. I knew God was a healer, but I didn't know anyone who had ever been healed.

It was the Wednesday before I was to enter the hospital. Gary and I got up and ate breakfast. Again we prayed together.

At about ten o'clock, as Gary was doing some chores around the house and I worked on bills at my desk in the solarium in our front foyer, the doorbell rang. Gary answered it. When he opened the door I heard a deep, melodious voice say, "I've come to tell Ann."

I turned to see a tall black man standing on the doorstep. He was taller than my six-foot-five-inch husband. His skin was ebony and his eyes were a deep, shimmering azure. He looked past Gary and fixed his gaze directly on me. "Ann," he said, "the cancer in your body has been healed."

"How do you know?" I managed to gasp.

"God told me," he answered.

I stared at him uncomprehendingly. I noticed his unusual clothing. He wore a loose, black, gossamer tunic with swirling golden threads, and dark, flowing trousers. His shoes were woven from some ribbonlike material. He was clean-shaven with close-cropped hair, and there was an aura of peace about him.

"Would you like to come in?" I said. I glanced at Gary, who was as awestruck as I. He stepped aside for the man to enter.

"Sir," I said, standing up, "I don't understand What is your name?"

He smiled radiantly and touched his left shoulder with the index and middle finger of his right hand. "My name is Thomas."

Speaking in the most comforting tones, Thomas told me I must not worry. He quoted Isaiah: ". . . and with his stripes we are healed." And then he said, "Before I go, I must pray for you."

He held out his right palm about twelve inches from my forehead. "Father God," he began, and as he prayed I felt intense heat radiating from his hand. My legs weakened, my eyes closed, and as I fell gently to the floor I was aware of a powerful white light moving up through my body.

I awoke to see Gary leaning over me. "Ann, are you all right?"

"Where is he?" I asked.

But Thomas had vanished.

I crawled to the phone and called my doctor. "Something has happened to me that I can't explain," I said. "I won't need the surgery."

The doctor said he realized how the stress and fear could be affecting my imagination. But I insisted. Finally we compromised. If I would show up for the surgery, he would perform another biopsy as I lay on the operating table before any further procedures were done.

I agreed. And that Sunday I entered the hospital as planned. When I awoke in my room afterward, my doctor was at my bedside shaking his head. "Ann, I can't explain it. Your tissue appears clean. We didn't operate. We'll do further tests, but for now you're in the clear."

In the years since, there has been no recurrence of the cancer. Thomas did not return. But no longer do I think of angels as confined to Christmas cards. I know that they are here among us, doing God's work in our lives.

"She's the One"

MARK MARQUEZ

om was a fixer. Whether it was as simple as sewing a button back on a pair of faded overalls for one of her eight children or repairing a broken tractor on the farm she ran single-handedly while holding down a full-time job, there was nothing she couldn't fix. And that included people too. I'd often come home from school in the afternoons to find her sitting with a stranger at the kitchen table, sipping the cup of coffee that was forever in her hand. "Who's that, Mom?" I'd ask once they'd gone. Mom would always take off her glasses, rub her eyes and say the same thing: "Just someone with a problem, who needed to talk." That's exactly who I was now, only Mom couldn't fix this problem for me.

Oh, she'd tried. On my wedding day, in particular. I'd been so careful with my new suit that morning. I had wanted everything to go perfectly: to settle down and make Mom proud. But I'd had second thoughts lately. The whole thing was happening so fast. And then my fiancée was late to the ceremony.

"She's not the one, Mark," Mom told me, standing there in a fancy dress. "It's not too late to call this off."

"But Mom! What about all the food? All those people?"

"Don't you worry," she said. "I can fix all that. The important thing is, she's not the one."

I knew Mom was right. But I was young and headstrong, and so eager to start a family of my own. I convinced my mother, and myself, that these were just cold feet. I went through with the wedding. Mom died of complications from diabetes a year later. My wife and I spent the next nine years trying to save the marriage we should never have rushed.

Now I was divorced, and my ex-wife and two children had moved clear across the state. Meanwhile I was barely making ends meet working as a mechanic in a factory. That's when I met Louise.

Louise had long blonde hair, soft eyes and a constant smile. Although what I first noticed about her was how easy she was to talk to. And we had plenty of time to talk, side by side, while I fixed the machines Louise worked on. It was the first time since Mom died that I'd found someone I could open up to. Louise was a great listener and, divorced with two kids herself, she really understood my problems. Soon we were eating lunch together in the cafeteria. Louise knew money was tight for me and would pretend to make too much lunch for herself "by accident." Our conversations were continuing well past quitting time. It didn't take long for me to realize I was in love. I felt like the luckiest man alive when Louise said she was in love with me too.

Louise and I spent all of our free time together, and eventually I introduced her to my family. But whenever Louise talked about marriage, I'd get nervous and change the subject. After the divorce I lost a lot of confidence in myself and my decisions. I knew Louise and I were right for each other; I'd never been so happy. She was my best friend. We could finish each other's sentences! But marriage had gone so badly for me before. *Maybe I'm just not cut out for that kind of life,* I thought. I needed an objective opinion. From someone I could trust. Someone who knew me. Someone who was used to giving good advice. Someone like Mom.

After Mom died, one of my brothers and I took over the farm, but my mother's house was sold out of the family. I'd taken Louise to the farm many times, but she'd never seen the home I grew up in. One day I went to see the new homeowner about some hay baling that needed to be done on his portion of the property. I took Louise with me. We walked up to Mom's old front porch, and I knocked on the door. No answer. I promised Louise we would come back another time to look around inside. As we turned to leave, Louise stopped.

"I've been here before," she said quietly, staring out across the field.

"What?" I asked.

"I've been here before! Or at least I have been in a dream. I was sitting right here, on these steps, and there was a woman with me—an older woman. She was wearing glasses and drinking a steaming cup of coffee."

Louise said she'd had the dream a while back, right after we started dating. She hadn't thought about it again until now. "It was evening, and there was a nice breeze. The woman and I sat together for a long while."

"Did she say anything to you?"

"That was the strange part," Louise replied. "She said, 'You're the one.' That's it. Otherwise we sat in silence."

From that day on I didn't get that nervous feeling when I thought about a future with Louise. I knew as if the words had come straight from Mom's lips: "She's the one." We've been married thirteen years. And besides the four children we had between us when we met, we've got two more. We have a farm as well and our own porch steps. Many times I've looked over at Louise sitting on those steps and realized how much like Mom she is. You see, Louise is a fixer too. She single-handedly fixed one man's broken heart. Well, with a little help from an angel, who came to her in a dream and said those three little words that only I would understand.

8

PROTECTING THE VULNERABLE

Angels, where'er we go,
Attend our steps whate'er betide.
With watchful care their charge defend,
And evil turn aside.
—CHARLES WESLEY

Something about that fourth line of poetry captures my attention and imagination: an angel defending its charges and turning aside evil—or physical harm. In an unseen realm it may happen more frequently than we ever know about. For reasons they may never understand, the writers in this section were allowed a behind-the-scenes glimpse or spiritual awareness of protection at moments when they or their loved ones were particularly vulnerable. We don't know why some accidents, crimes or disasters are averted and others aren't. Even so, we have reason to be grateful for every protection afforded us by angels keeping watch day or night.

Angel in the House

BONNIE WILSON

By now the kids and I were used to Steve's being on the road. His trucker job sometimes kept him away for a month at a time. We were glad to have him home for Christmas, but just after New Year's he had to go again. Steve loved his job. But that didn't make it any easier for him to say good-bye.

"I think about you when I'm out there," he said as he hugged me at dawn that January morning. "I pray for God to watch over you all. Sometimes it doesn't feel like enough."

"Don't you worry yourself."

The kids and I quickly fell into our daily routine without Steve. But nights were another story. One cold Monday I got ready for bed. I imagined Steve driving along a stretch of roadway. I wished he was home with us instead.

I walked into the girls' room. Kimberly, ten, and Carrie, eight, were ready for bed. "How about I sleep in here tonight?" I asked.

"What about Ray?" said Carrie.

Their brother Ray's room was right next to the girls' with a connecting door between the two. *Yes, Ray should be here with us.*

What a strange thought. Ray was twelve, almost a teenager. He would not want any part of this. *Ask him.*

I stuck my head through the doorway. Ray was sitting up in bed. "We're all sleeping in here tonight," I said. "Why don't you join us? Come on, it'll be fun."

Ray thought about it. "Okay," he said. "If you want."

The four of us got settled in. "This is kind of nice, all of us together like this, isn't it?" The kids and I traded jokes and talked about what Steve might be doing. He'd called home earlier from a truck stop in Missouri. *Lord, keep him safe on the road,* I asked. No matter where he was, I knew Steve's prayer was the mirror opposite of mine: "Lord, keep my family safe at home." I said good-night to the kids and shut off the light.

It was still dark when I woke up. Someone was shaking me. "Kim?" I murmured. "Go back to sleep."

Kim shook me again and pointed at the open door to Ray's room. I sat up. I rubbed my eyes, straining to see. Something was in the doorway. *What is that?* In the dim light I could make out a tall figure. *With wings?* The figure had one hand on the door frame. The other motioned us out. An angel was telling us to leave the house. *Why?*

I craned my neck to look past the angel into Ray's room. The walls were alive with an orange glow. *Fire?* I couldn't see any smoke. I didn't smell smoke. But the room was definitely on fire. And then I realized: The angel was holding back the flames and smoke.

"Kids, wake up! We have to get out." The kids jumped out of bed, grabbed blankets, and we all hurried outside.

A policeman met us at the door. A fire truck came screaming up the street. When I looked back at the house I saw the kids' bedrooms in flames. The windows exploded and the fire roared out. *We barely made it,* I thought.

The kids and I went to my parents' house, and I left word with Steve's trucking company about what had happened and where we were. "Thank goodness you were awake," my mom said as we got the kids settled down.

"Kim woke me," I said. "She pointed at—" I looked over at Kim, already asleep. Had she seen the angel too? Could I have imagined it? "Kim pointed at the fire," I finished.

Next morning we learned that the fire had started in the light switch on the porch, traveled up through the wires and burned through the wall in Ray's room. That's where the flames had first appeared. I drove over to take a look. The kids' rooms were gutted, the walls black and charred. The ceiling had burned away, leaving a few beams and the roof above it. Nothing was salvageable. Then I saw our Bible, the pages unburned. I took it with me when I left.

When I got back to my parents' house Kim was waiting to talk to me. "Mom?" she asked. "Did you see anything strange in our room last night when you woke up?"

My heart beat a little faster, but I didn't want to influence Kim's story with my own. "What did you see?"

"I think I saw an angel," Kim said, "standing in the doorway holding back the fire."

I gave Kim a hug. "I saw it too."

Steve drove home from Missouri without stopping. I threw my arms around him. "I'm just sorry I wasn't here to protect you. I meant to ask," he said, "what was Ray doing sleeping in the girls' room?"

I remembered my strange urge to ask Ray to sleep with us.

"Thank God," said Steve. "He heard my prayers."

Steve's back on the road now. But I sleep just fine. It's still hard for us to say good-bye, but Steve and I both know he doesn't have to be at home for us to be safe. Our prayers are always enough.

Between a Tractor and a Tree Stump

NORRIS MCPIKE

ack in May of 1998 I found myself between jobs. I spent a lot of time on the "minifarm" my wife, Bonnie, and I owned. That's what I called our acreage, even though nothing much grew there. Except trees.

One spot was thick with them, some reaching as high as fifty feet. They were getting too big. It wouldn't be long till they got some kind of disease or their roots could not provide them with enough food. They would end up sick and dying. That's why I needed to harvest them. I'd miss their beauty, but their wood would be put to good use as lumber.

Before Bonnie headed off to work in town one morning, I told her, "I think I'm gonna get around to felling some of those trees today. I should be done by the time you get home at four." I don't usually do logging jobs on my own, but that day I just got the itch to do it. My new job started in less than a month, and I wanted to take care of things while I still had the time. I could handle it.

I drove the tractor out to the area I wanted to clear. I fired up my chainsaw and got to cutting. Tree after tree came down. Everything went smoothly, till the last tree. This one was huge, wider around than two or three of me put together and so tall I could barely see the top. I set to sawing, stopping every once in a while to catch my breath and mop my brow. Finally, with a great creaking, the tree started to lean. Slowly at first. Then it picked up speed as it gave way. It smashed right smack on top of another tree, bending it down toward the ground. I had to get the tree I'd cut down off the one still planted. *This is gonna be tough,* I thought. *I'll need a chain long enough to wrap around it and strong enough to wrench it loose and lift it up.*

I went to the shed to check if I had any chains. I found only one, and it looked a bit short for the purpose I had in mind. I glanced at my watch: 2:00 PM.

I really want to get this done before Bonnie gets home, I thought. I decided to try using the chain anyway. Might be able to do it. I went back to the field and wrapped the chain around the trunk of the fallen tree. It fit, so I hooked the other end to the tractor. Gave it a few good tugs. It held.

I climbed up onto the seat and started the engine. Pressed down on the gas pedal ever so slightly. This had to go at a slow pace. I turned to look over my shoulder. So far, so good. Then, all of a sudden, there was a snapping of wood. The branches on the living tree moved and then sprung up. The chained tree went flying, as if shot from a catapult. It flew toward me just like a missile.

Jump! I thought. But there wasn't time. Instinctively, I grabbed the steering wheel tight, ducked my head and hung on. Everything went black.

When I came to, my head was jammed up against the stump of one of the trees I'd cut down earlier. My bottom jaw was being pushed to the side. Much more than it should have. And the tractor was upside down on top of me. Something hard dug into my back. *Must be the gear shift,* I thought. I tried to move my arms, but I couldn't. They were pinned. How long had I been out? The watch on my left wrist faced away from me. I wriggled and twisted and it moved just enough so I could see that it was 2:15 PM. *You've been out fifteen minutes.*

Why had I tried this on my own? No one but Bonnie knew where I was, and she wouldn't get back for hours. The pain in my back worsened. The tractor seemed to grow heavier. Would it snap me in half or just crush me down farther into the earth?

Dear Lord, I prayed, *looks like this is it. You want to take me home now. If that's your plan, it's fine with me. But please, please, take away the pain.*

I saw something out of the corner of my eye. I strained to see and made out two figures standing nearby, looking at me. Strong figures in white, flowing robes. One of them spoke. "What should we do now?" he said.

It was the strangest thing because his lips never moved, but in my head I heard him. Then I noticed, right next to the tractor, two pairs of feet, one on either side of a tractor tire. The tire rose up unexpectedly till it was about four inches off the ground. The pressure on my body eased. My back didn't hurt as bad. My eyelids grew heavy. Soon I drifted off, not into unconsciousness but into a deep, restful sleep.

I woke to Bonnie shouting my name. She must have come looking for me when she got home and saw the tractor still gone. But I couldn't take a deep enough breath to shout back. I guess she finally saw the upturned tractor. She came running. "Norris, are you okay?"

"Get help!" I gasped. While she was gone I looked for the angels. I couldn't see them anymore. But I felt their presence. At least the two who'd been closest to me. I noticed the tractor tire still above the ground. About four inches. *They're still here! Thank you, Lord.*

Bonnie came back a while later with my brother-in-law and a friend. They used a jack to lift the tractor enough so I could breathe more freely. The fire department came with some large air bags. They put them all around me under the tractor and then filled them with compressed air. The tractor slowly lifted. Finally there was enough room for the EMTs to get to me. They loaded me into a medical helicopter and flew me to the hospital.

Doctors examined me and found I had a broken rib, as well as a severe burn on my back. It hadn't been the gear shift pressing into me after all; acid from the battery had leaked and dripped onto me! Plus, my left ear had been torn nearly all the way off. "You're lucky to be alive," they told me. But I was alive. Yes, I'd been dumb to work on my own like that, but God didn't hold it against me. He sent his angels anyway. They helped me then, and I know they'll be around if I ever need them again.

Deer Crossing

PATRICE VACCA

*M*oving from urban New Jersey to the Pennsylvania woods was a dream come true for me. The land around my house was a campground in the summer. My nearest neighbor was miles away, and there was no phone service to my house. Didn't bother me a bit.

Back in New Jersey I'd worked as a rehab nurse. I saw people all the time. Some predicted I would soon tire of my new solitary life, but I hadn't so far and didn't expect I ever would. All my life I've felt connected to nature, and I could never feel lonely with animals nearby. The woods were full of them.

"I call that one Scarbelly," I told a visiting friend when a deer tiptoed out of the woods one afternoon. She was a doe, easily recognizable by the old wound running from her shoulder to her hip. "She had a fawn last year. She brings her baby around too."

"They sure seem to like you a lot!" she said as the doe inched nearer to me. We stayed very still so as not to startle her.

"I'd like to think so," I said. "Deer aren't easy to get close to."

Each day I woke up in my house in the woods was a pleasure—until one April morning. I heard the birds singing as usual, saw the pale sun through the window, smelled the fresh air. But something was wrong. I tried to sit up. My legs felt like lead. They refused to cooperate with me. I had to struggle just to swing them over the side of the bed.

I managed to stand. *Get to the bathroom,* I thought. Just turning in the right direction almost knocked me over I was so off-balance. I managed to shuffle toward the bathroom door.

Thud.

My shoulder hit the doorjamb. How could I miss the door? I took a step back and tried another time. Once again my shoulder hit the door.

I didn't feel it at all. In fact, I couldn't feel my shoulder, my arm, my fingers on the left side of my body. It was like a great emptiness hung where my arm should be. I tried to squeeze my fingers together. They wouldn't budge.

Stroke! I thought, my nurse training kicking in. My mother and grandmother had both died from strokes. Could that be happening to me—at forty-six? I had to get to a hospital fast. But how? No neighbors, no phone . . .

"Well, God," I mumbled, "we've got to do something here. I need help!"

I pulled on the easiest clothes I could find and slipped my feet into sandals. I moved carefully to the door.

"Scarbelly!"

The old doe was waiting on the deck. Her fawn stood at her side. Four more deer crowded behind them.

They weren't the rescue team I'd imagined, but they were all I had. "Look, I have to get to a doctor," I said. "Now."

The deer flicked their ears, watching.

If I could just get to the road at the top of the hill, I thought, *I could flag someone down.* Could I make it that far? I had to try. The longer I went untreated, the worse the damage could be.

I moved stiffly off the deck and onto the lawn, forcing my left side to move. The deer were close behind me.

The lawn stretched out before me like an ocean. I'll never make it all that way!

I put my hand to my face, ready to cry. *That won't help!* I told myself. I rubbed my eyes and looked down at the gravel road. I was standing at the edge of it. I looked over my shoulder at the expanse of lawn and my house in the distance. *How in the world did I get here?* I didn't remember walking that significant distance—and it would have taken ages. But here I was and so were the deer—right beside me. Scarbelly's deep brown eyes looked into mine. "Did you carry me?" I said.

She blinked her long lashes. She was so close I could have touched her.

A cloud of dust in the distance! I waved frantically as the car got closer. The driver smiled and waved back at me, but he didn't even slow down. He couldn't even tell I needed help!

Another car went by. The same thing happened. Again and again.

"I have to go out to the middle of the road," I said. "They'll either stop or run me over. If I don't get help, I might not make it anyway."

I pulled myself into the road. The herd of deer walked forward, keeping pace with my own tortured steps. They huddled close around me, surrounding me with a protective circle in the middle of the road. The heat from their bodies warmed me. Their soft sides rose and fell in a calming rhythm. I felt their gentle breath on my skin.

A truck appeared in the distance, moving toward us. *If this one doesn't stop, I don't know what I'll do.*

I raised my hand and held it straight out in front of me. The deer stood still as stone, not budging even as the truck came at full speed. Thank goodness, it slowed and stopped. The driver stuck his head out of the window and stared at me, a woman surrounded by a herd of deer.

"Please," I said, "I need to get to the hospital. I think I had a stroke."

The driver's eyes moved to the deer and back to me. He opened his mouth, but no words came out. He shook his head and climbed out of the truck, hurrying to open the passenger door.

The deer parted to let me get to the truck. The driver eyed them the whole time he helped me inside. The deer eyed him too, but they didn't run away as they usually did when faced with people. People besides me, that is. The driver got me safe in the passenger seat and got behind the wheel. He shifted into gear and beeped the horn as gently as he could. Only then did the deer lower their heads and step gracefully off the road.

I lay my head against the car seat, exhausted. *Thank you, God,* I prayed, *for your beautiful creatures who watched over me like you do.*

Tests at the hospital proved I had had a stroke. "You should have a good recovery," the doctor told me. "You're lucky you were able to get here as quickly as you did. If you'd waited, you might have had serious long-term damage."

I might have been lucky, but the situation was nothing short of angelic.

Stranger at the Station

JULIA GOODWORTH SABOL

There were no signs of life outside the station as I squinted through the rain. I stepped off the bus with my suitcase over my head and made a run for it. Inside the heavy entrance door I found myself all alone in the huge terminal where I had to change buses. Deserted. That's how I felt no matter where I was these days.

I hadn't always felt that way. Since I was a little girl I'd been certain angels were watching over me every moment. Like the time someone whispered for me to wake up in the middle of the night and saved my whole family from a fire in our home. But where had that reassuring voice been when the doctor told me the child I was expecting would never come into this world? I took a trip to visit my family, hoping to find some peace. Now I was on my way back to my husband, but my heart was just as heavy as the day I left. God had always been there to guard against tragedy. Where was he now?

I looked around the waiting room, but saw only shadows, no people. It was one o'clock in the morning. Yet somewhere there was music playing. I followed the sound to a lunch counter at the other end of the terminal. A gruff-looking man was reading a newspaper. Apparently he was both the cook and the ticket agent.

"How long before the next bus to Petersburg?" I asked.

The man scowled up at the grease-covered clock on the wall. "Couple of hours," he mumbled, going back to his paper.

I returned to the dimly lit waiting area. There were rows of empty wooden benches. I found one near enough light to read and pulled out my book. I'd only read a few lines when I sensed I was no longer alone.

Seven young men sat directly opposite me. Each one sat with his arms crossed, staring at me. I pulled my cardigan tightly around my shoulders, hoping another bus had arrived with more travelers. No, it was just me and this gang of men—and they weren't travelers. They were obviously here to start trouble, and there was no one to protect me from them.

Hands shaking, I closed my book and stood up. The gang stood up too. The lunch counter seemed miles away. I couldn't hear the music anymore. My heart beat so loudly I thought I would faint. I stepped away from my seat.

Footsteps behind me got louder—and closer. *Dear God, help me!*

A man appeared at the end of the row of benches. "There you are!" he exclaimed. I looked up into his smiling, handsome face. My heartbeat slowed. I'd never seen him before, but somehow he knew I needed help. "I've been waiting ages for you!" he said. "I was afraid you'd gotten lost."

The stranger was about forty years old with a strong, sturdy build—he looked like Superman! He picked up my suitcase with little effort and threw his free arm around my trembling shoulders. "Let's have a cup of coffee while we wait for your bus."

I didn't look back. By the time the stranger and I got to the lunch counter, the gang was gone. The man behind the register perked up and brewed us a fresh pot of coffee. My companion didn't touch his cup, but we chatted until it was time for my next bus.

Dawn was arriving as he held open the station's heavy door for me. The storm was over, and my bus waited across the still-damp blacktop. As I got onboard, the stranger handed me my suitcase. I looked down to thank him, but he wasn't there.

As the bus pulled out, I thought about all the sadness I'd experienced over the past few weeks and thanked God for the angel who came to my rescue. God hadn't deserted me. He was watching over me still, just like when I was a girl. And that knowledge would see me through the many joys—and trials—of life.

Only Human?

JESS PRUITT

Same name as me? What were the chances of that? But there I was on my CB radio, talking to another trucker named Jess. Good thing too; talking to him kept me awake. I was on my way home and so tired that night, I could hardly keep my eyes open. I rolled the window down, drank some water, ate a piece of candy. Nothing worked. I didn't like to bother God about little things, but this time I was desperate. So I asked.

That's when this guy came over the CB radio. We introduced ourselves. "I drive for your company," he said. "I'm headed for the terminal in Lafayette."

That was my destination too. Same name, same company, same destination? We had so much in common. I couldn't wait to meet him when I got off the road. We talked for over an hour. Before I knew it, we were nearing Lafayette. What a relief! I'd soon be home.

I lost track of Jess on my CB, but I figured I'd see him at the terminal. I sure wanted to say thanks for all he'd done. I waited in my semi for a while, but he didn't show up, so I walked inside and checked with the office. Maybe Jess had been there already looking for me.

"I know all the drivers in this company," the clerk said. "You're the only Jess there is." I guess it's okay to pray to the Lord for even the smallest things. I'd asked for help, and I got it.

Prepared

LORI A. KENNEDY

*I*ndependent, that's me. If someone offers help, my automatic response is, "I can do it." This can dent my husband's ego, but I like to think he's glad I can take care of myself. For example, I'm ready for all kinds of weather. Northern California, where we live, isn't the land of sunny beaches. We have snow in winter, especially up here, 2,400 feet high in the Sierra Nevada foothills. We are out of cell-phone range, and there are no houses nearby. We can be cut off from the world if the power goes out during a storm! So my cupboard is well stocked with water, canned goods and extra batteries. I ride around with emergency supplies in the trunk of my car, including hiking boots and granola bars. Like the Girl Scout I was for many years, my motto is "Be Prepared."

A warm, sunny day in early November came as a nice surprise. "I'm going Christmas shopping!" I announced. My husband stayed behind to rake the last of the autumn leaves. "Russ," I shouted, backing out of the garage, "call me if you think of anything you want from town."

The town of Chico was in the valley, twenty miles away. It was even warmer there, and I enjoyed myself walking from store to store. I noticed the sun fading, but I kept shopping. It was nearly six o'clock when I loaded up the trunk with my packages. *Why haven't I heard from Russ?* I wondered. He usually thought of something he wanted while I was in town. I pulled my cell phone out of my purse. *Oops.* It was turned off. I dialed our number. Russ answered on the first ring.

"I've been trying to reach you," he said. "Believe it or not, it's snowing up here!"

"The forecast was for clear weather," I protested. "I guess I'll put the chains on to get home."

Russ cleared his throat. "Uh, you can't do that," he said. "I forgot to put them back in the trunk after I vacuumed the car yesterday."

I clenched my teeth. "How long has it been snowing?"

"Half an hour or so," he said.

"I can make it." I hung up and threw the cell phone back in my purse. *How could he have been so careless?* Never mind. My can-do attitude kicked into gear.

The roads were clear till I reached 1,200 feet. Big tufts of snow swirled in front of the headlights. Drifts mounted by the roadside. I kept the car in low gear, creeping slowly upward. The windshield wipers swept away snow in clumps. I could barely see, but I knew I'd soon reach the bridge across the lake. After crossing, all I had to do was climb the steep hill three miles from our house. "You know what you're doing," I told myself. "You can do this." I couldn't call Russ even if I'd wanted to. I was out of range.

The snow was falling heavily by the time I reached the bridge. There was a truck ahead of me. *Hurrah!* Those big tires made a nice path through the snow. But the truck stopped when it reached the end of the bridge, and I had to stop too. The driver got out, swept the snow from his windshield, and then got back in and drove away. I'd lost precious momentum when I stopped the car. "Don't chicken out now," I said to myself. I started up the hill. The car swerved. Left, then right. "Come on! Come on!" I couldn't get control of the car. My tires spun. The car slid backward. "Help," I cried. "God, please help me!" There was nothing on either side of the road but a slippery slope into the water.

I took my foot off the gas pedal. The car chugged and came to an abrupt stop. Someone tapped on my window. I nearly jumped out of the driver's seat. Another tap. I caught my breath and rolled the window down. A tall man with dark, curly hair stood in the falling snow.

"You'll never make it up this hill, ma'am," he said. "Better to walk. I'll push your car to the side of the road. You steer." I nodded and turned off the engine. I had no choice but to accept help from this dark-haired stranger. I doubted he'd be able to budge the car an inch. I could easily hike up to the gas station at the top of the hill and use their phone to call Russ to come get me.

Before I had the window rolled back up, I was moving. My car seemed to float over the snow! I steered to the edge of the road.

The man came to the window again. He didn't look so strong. "Don't forget your Christmas packages in the trunk," he said. *How does he know I've been Christmas shopping?*

I grabbed a flashlight from the glove compartment and stepped out of the car. The snow had tapered off. "Hello," I said, shining the light around me. But the man was already gone. I shone the light down on the snow. No footprints leading anywhere. Odd, but no time to wonder. At least I had my boots in the trunk. I pulled them on, grabbed my packages and trudged toward the gas station. I didn't want Russ coming down here to look for me.

Another setback: The station was closed. I leaned against the building and sighed. It was cold. I was exhausted. How could I possibly walk three miles home? "Well," I said to myself, "where's your can-do attitude now?" So I started walking. At least the snow had stopped.

I was startled to see my shadow stretching in front of me. Headlights were coming up behind. I watched as a white pickup approached. The driver rolled down his window. It was the dark-haired man. "Like a ride home?"

"Would I!" I shouted. "I'm three miles from here." I went around to the passenger side and shoved my shopping bags on the floor. The man held out his hand and pulled me up onto the seat.

I rearranged the bags at my feet. When I looked up we were at my house already. "Oh my gosh," I said. I gathered my packages and got out of the truck. "How can I ever thank you?"

"Just go inside and get warm," he replied. By the time I walked up the three steps to our deck, the man had driven away.

Russ was surprised to see me at the door. "I didn't hear your car," he said. I told him what had happened. "But I didn't hear a truck either," he said.

That didn't make sense. We walked to the end of the deck. A smooth blanket of deep snow covered the driveway and the road leading to it. We saw no tire tracks. Not one mark.

There are many ways to be prepared. I was a pro at the obvious ones. But an emergency is more than you can ever prepare for on your own. An emergency demands asking for help. Especially from the One who's always prepared to give it.

9

GIVING GIFTS
TO CHILDREN

And the voice of God spoke, saying: Of all the gifts of
all the angels, I find that this small box pleases me most.
—CHARLES TAZEWELL, *The Littlest Angel*

As a child I loved the Christmas story of *The Littlest Angel,* who gave his most precious keepsakes—a bird's egg, his dog's collar—to God to honor the birth of the Christchild. God was so pleased with his gift that he made it shine as brightly as . . . the Bethlehem star. It's an imaginative fictional tale, but the memory of it lingers, pleasantly reminding me of the generosity of the heavenly beings as orchestrated by God.

Our stories in this section of the angelic procession focus on gifts given to children throughout the year. Being a baseball fan, I particularly like Tom Elliott's "Tickets from Heaven." A different favorite might inspire you to perform some act of kindness to make life a little easier for some child in your life.

Poochy 'n' Me

JO GROSSMAN

wo miles separated my house from Carver's General Store, but I didn't mind the trip when Poochy was with me. I pedaled my J. C. Higgins bike down Graham Road. Poochy always ran right alongside me, round velvety ears flapping, pink tongue hanging out. Poochy was my best friend that summer in the 1940s. My only friend. I was eleven. Dad lived in a mental hospital fifty miles away. Mom worked long hours and didn't make enough for someone to babysit me. I was on my own. Mom always said God was with me, but I sure couldn't feel it. My nighttime prayers seemed to go nowhere.

I figured God had more important things to do than listen to me. Not like Poochy, who never left my side.

Poochy slept at the foot of my bed. We roamed the woods behind our house together. He stood lookout while I raided my neighbor's cherry tree and lay beside me as I read mysteries under the old apple tree.

I pedaled up to Carver's and leaned my bike against the side. "You wait here, Poochy, while I get us some ice cream."

Poochy wagged his feathery tail. I always shared my vanilla cup with him.

In the store, Mr. Carver was slicing meat for a customer. I'd have to wait. I glanced out the window for a sight of Poochy's black-and-tan head and remembered the spring morning two years before when I'd first found him in Mom's flower garden. Just a scruffy cocker-spaniel-sized dog with big brown eyes and floppy ears lying in the purple tulips. "You look hungry," I'd said.

Poochy had thumped his tail and looked up at me sadly. I climbed into the flowers and sat beside him. His hair was matted and his paws were sore. He looked just as lonely as I was.

When Mom got home from work, I begged her to let me keep him. "You know I don't have time to take care of a dog, Judy," Mom said.

"I'll take care of him all by myself. I promise!" I told her.

Mom looked doubtfully at the mutt at my side. Poochy offered her his paw. Mom didn't stand a chance. She dropped to her knees and shook the paw. "I guess you're old enough to take care of a dog," she said. "But he's going to need a collar." Mom drove me to Woolworth on Front Street and let me pick out a bright red collar from the sale rack.

"You're really mine now, Poochy," I said as I fastened the collar on him. "That's what I'm going to call you."

Poochy thumped his tail happily.

I could just imagine him thumping his tail right now as he waited for his ice cream. I quickly paid for my cup and hurried out to the front steps.

But Poochy wasn't there.

"Poochy?" I called. "Poochy! Here, boy! Where'd you go?"

There was no answer. *He probably just wandered away,* I thought, but fear squeezed my heart. I dropped my ice cream. "Poochy!" I ran to the middle of Graham Road and looked both ways. I checked the wooded area and creek around back of the store. No Poochy.

He went home, I thought. *He must have gone home.*

I jumped on my bike and pedaled as fast as I could, searching for Poochy through tear-blurred eyes. But Poochy wasn't waiting when I got home. I called his name over and over, but no happy bark called back in response.

I dialed Mom at work. "He might have run off after a squirrel," she said when I managed to choke out the story. "If he's not home tonight we'll make up a notice. Why don't you ride back to the store and see if Mr. Carver's seen him?"

I sped back to the store and burst through the front door. "Have you seen my dog?" I blurted out to Mr. Carver.

"No, Judy, I haven't," he said.

I stumbled outside and collapsed on the front steps crying.

"What's wrong?" A woman in a blue dress smiled kindly down at me.

"I lost my dog."

"Have you looked hard for him?"

"I looked everywhere!" I cried. "He's brown and black and has a red collar. I don't know what to do."

"Have you asked God to help you find him?" the woman in blue asked.

I wiped the tears off my cheeks with the back of my hand. "God's too busy to look for my dog."

"God cares about all his creatures," the lady said. "He cares about you and your dog. His love has no limit. Why don't you talk to him?"

The lady went down the steps to her car and drove away. I wasn't sure I should believe her about God's love, but I had no one else to turn to.

I bowed my head like Mom taught me. "God, please bring Poochy back to me. I miss him so much." Once I started talking to God, I couldn't stop. I told him how lonely I was. Somehow it seemed like my prayers were going straight to God's ear, like he was really listening, as if he were sitting right there with me on the steps of Carver's General Store.

I pedaled home and sat in the swing under the apple tree, waiting for Mom. I heard a car in the driveway and ran around to the front.

It wasn't Mom. It was a car I'd never seen before. A man got out, walked around to the passenger side and opened the door. Something furry jumped out and hurtled toward me.

"Poochy!" I threw my arms around him. Poochy thumped his tail. "Hey, Mister, where did you find my dog?"

The stranger hung his head sheepishly. "I took him from outside Carver's store. Had him tied to a tree in my yard when some lady came to my door. She gave me a hard time. Said he belonged to a little girl. She made me feel bad so I drove back to Carver's store. He told me where you lived."

"The lady who talked to you," I said. "Was she wearing a blue dress?"

"Yeah," the man answered. "You know that lady?"

I shook my head.

The man ducked back into his car. "Sorry about your dog," he muttered.

I watched the man drive away, hugging Poochy in my arms. I had my friend with me again. I also had God, right there beside me. Thanks to a mysterious lady in blue who told me exactly how to find them both.

Gently Swinging

JACKIE DONHAM

*D*arling Misty. She looked so lost in the big baby bed. Her red, puckered face poked out from under a white blanket. Her tiny hands grasped feebly at the air. I touched my palm to her forehead. It was hot, probably another fever. I lifted her onto my lap and put a warm bottle to her lips. Her heart beat softly against my chest. Her lips closed around the nipple, but she was too weak to suck. I stroked her cheek and felt her swallow a single drop of formula. I looked at the clock. Four AM. It was going to be a long night.

If I hadn't been an LPN, my husband, Ray, and I never would have considered taking in a foster baby like Misty. Born to alcoholic parents, she had an immune deficiency. She'd been a two-pound preemie and only weighed seven pounds when we got her at five months old. Her lungs and trachea were damaged from being on a respirator. Sometimes it took five hours a day to get enough formula down her to survive, and it was a monumental task for her to gain even a single pound. But from the very first moment I held Misty at the foster agency, I knew that God meant me to take care of her, even if I was fifty.

I drifted off only to wake to the sound of Misty crying. I stood up stiffly and paced the hallway, cooing softly in her ear. For the past week, Misty couldn't sleep more than an hour at a time. And when she woke up, so did I. I was not sure how much longer I could go at this rate.

Finally Misty quieted. I laid her in bed, checked her apnea monitor and put my hand on her chest to feel her breathing. I was afraid to leave her, even for a minute, so I pulled up a chair and settled down to catch some rest.

The next time I woke up, it was light outside. Misty was crying. I picked her up and changed her diaper. I could hear Ray in the bathroom getting ready for his day at Fort Knox. He appeared, dressed for work, and kissed Misty and me good-bye. He stopped and looked at us with concern.

"You sure you'll be okay today, Jackie?" he asked. "You look done in."

"Oh, I'm getting used to it," I said, forcing a smile. I was afraid that if Ray knew how exhausted I was, he'd try to take a sick day. He'd taken too many of those lately. "We'll be fine," I assured him. Misty and I walked him to the door.

"Don't forget, the social worker's coming this afternoon," Ray called out from the driveway. I had forgotten.

Of all days, Lord...

I slumped down onto the couch, staring around the living room. The floors needed vacuuming, unread newspapers littered the coffee table. There were dirty dishes piled in the kitchen sink, the hamper in the bathroom was overflowing, and the bed wasn't made. I was almost afraid to look at myself in the mirror; it had been so long since I'd done anything with my hair.

What would the social worker think if she saw our house in this state? We could lose Misty. *Lord, you put her in my care. Why, if she can't rely on me?*

Misty had fallen asleep on my chest. I stood up slowly so as not to wake her. Just as I went to lay her in bed, she coughed. Then cried. I put her up over my shoulder and rubbed her back. Her cries turned into wails. My legs felt like jelly underneath me, and each of Misty's screams bore into my head. *Lord, I have to find some way to soothe her!*

The old battery-operated baby swing my friend had lent me! It had put Misty to sleep before. Maybe it would work now. Cradling Misty with one hand, I pulled the swing out of the closet and moved it into the living room. I laid her down in the seat and tucked in a blanket around her. I turned the switch to "on." The power light stayed dark. I flicked the switch back and forth. My heart sank. We hadn't replaced the batteries. I checked the utility drawer, looking for another set. Misty screamed from the living room. I ran back to her. "I'm sorry, little one." The baby's cry reached a new shrill pitch. Tears sprang to my eyes.

"God," I pleaded, "I don't know what to do. I feel old and tired." I pushed the swing back and forth with my hand. "Please help me." I took my hand off the swing—it rocked steadily, on its own.

Misty suddenly stopped crying. Her face brightened. She reached up, as if to wrap her tiny hand around the finger of some unseen being. A sleepy smile spread across her face. Her whole body relaxed. She gave a yawn, then rubbed her eyes and fell asleep in the gently rocking swing.

I picked up the toys and empty coffee mugs in the living room, put some laundry away, made the bed and did the dishes as quietly as possible. Then I ran a shower, leaving the door ajar in case Misty woke up. All that I heard from the living room was the steady, comforting creak of the swing.

I finished my shower and changed into fresh clothes, ready for the social worker. Misty was still sleeping, gently swinging, and I thanked God for a whole hour of peace. I guess all the old swing needed was a jump-start. *Like me!* I thought.

Was that all? I bent down by the swing. The power light was off. Looking closely, I noticed that the switch was clearly turned to the "off" setting. There was no way the swing could have been working on its own. I reached out my hand to keep the swing rocking and then stopped myself. Another hand was rocking Misty now. The same hand I could always rely on to steady me.

Christmas Will Find You

DEBRA S. BEHNKE

Christmas Eve I woke up early for our big family dinner. Dozens of relatives were due to arrive in a matter of hours, and of course there was lots to do. I went to the kitchen to put in the turkey. But first I took a deep breath. I had a special Christmas request I didn't want to forget. A prayer not so much for me and our guests, but for my teenage son Darryl. *Please, God,* I asked, *let us spend Christmas at home and not in the hospital.*

Darryl was born with spina bifida, a disease that affects the spinal column and nervous system, and hydrocephalus, which causes water to accumulate on the brain. As an infant, he had a shunt implanted in his head to make it easier to drain the fluid that accumulated, and throughout his young life he visited the children's hospital regularly. The doctors and nurses saw us almost as much as they saw their own families. Any day or night might include a surprise trip to the ER. Holidays were no exception. Not even Christmas Eve.

I don't want today ruined, I thought, wrapping a few last-minute presents at the kitchen table. *Darryl deserves a real Christmas more than any boy I know. Watching the Greenbay Packers play on television. Talking with Grandpa about the latest Nascar race. Teasing his younger sister*

Marianne. Just enjoying being a teenager on Christmas. My prayer went on and on through several bastings of the turkey. After laying it all out for God, I was more convinced than ever that Darryl deserved this day at home with his family.

Our doorbell rang and then rang again. The house filled with family and friends, sitting around, chatting and laughing, sipping on cider as holiday tunes hummed in the background. Darryl joked with Marianne. They helped me set the table. Everything was going perfectly. At dinner my father said grace. "Thank you, Lord, for filling this house with the Christmas spirit!" he said.

I looked over at Darryl. He was in trouble. *The shunt is malfunctioning!* I jumped out of my chair to help, but Darryl passed out, his face falling forward on the table.

My father got him into the car, and we raced to the hospital. We all knew the routine. Not a minute was wasted. We'd been through this a hundred times before. But still, this time was different. Today was Christmas Eve. The roads were empty. People were at home celebrating. *Why, Lord? Why today? Why can't Darryl have a real Christmas?*

In no time my son was prepped and in the operating theater, where doctors would repair the shunt. I sat in the waiting room. My parents and Marianne waited with me. We waited all night and into the morning. *Some Christmas,* I thought, flipping through a magazine. I tossed it onto the coffee table. A small tree sat in the corner of the room. A nice gesture on the part of the hospital staff, but it only reminded me of the Christmas Darryl was missing at home. *Lord, I wanted him to have a special holiday.*

Finally one of the nurses brought us good news. "Darryl's out of surgery, and he's just fine," she said. "He's resting comfortably in his room."

Dad squeezed my hand. "You go home and freshen up. We'll stay here with Darryl till you get back."

It was already daylight, I realized, when I got out to the parking lot. I drove home to the empty house. No family and friends, no fresh-baked desserts, no carols playing in the background. *Sorry I couldn't give you Christmas, Darryl,* I thought as I grabbed some clean clothes from his room. *Maybe next year.*

I showered, changed and drove back to the hospital. It was still eerily quiet. People were at home where they were supposed to be. I didn't run into a single doctor or nurse on my way to Darryl's room. But when I got there a man was coming out. Not just any man—but Santa Claus himself. *Aren't you a little late?* I thought. Christmas was practically over. It had come and gone, and we missed it. Darryl missed it. Despite my prayers. We didn't need some late Santa to rub it in.

Darryl and Marianne laughed inside the room. I heard the distinct crinkle of wrapping paper.

"Merry Christmas," Santa bellowed in my face, and surprised me with a hug. I could feel his coat, made of a rich red velvet. I'd never felt a Santa Claus outfit so plush—the cuffs seemed to be pure cashmere. He released me from his comforting arms and winked at me, his eyes sparkling with joy. His cheeks were rosy, his face vibrant, just like the Santas I remembered from childhood. But his snow-white beard had to be real. Who was this Santa?

He sauntered off down the hall, the picture of Christmas itself. What was going on here? Why did I feel like it was Christmas Eve all over again? In the hospital room I found Darryl and his sister sitting on the bed, surrounded by piles of shiny wrapping paper. Talk about Christmas spirit!

"Look what I got!" Marianne yelled, holding up a jewelry box. It was the exact same jewelry box she had asked for, but I wasn't able to find it anywhere at the mall. *How on earth did Santa get his hands on it?*

Darryl showed off a model of Dale Earnhardt's race car—Earnhardt happened to be Darryl's Nascar hero. And a Greenbay Packers sweatshirt. That was Darryl's favorite team. But how could Santa have known? No one at the hospital could explain our strange but wonderful visit. It was as if Santa had come just for us.

It wasn't the Christmas I'd prayed for. It wasn't what I wanted for Darryl. It was even better. It was the Christmas we would always remember. The Christmas that proved that wherever we are during the holiday season—in our homes surrounded by friends and family, or sitting in the hospital with a sick child—the spirit of Christ's love and mercy is always with us. No matter where we are, Christmas will always find us.

They Call Him Kangaroo Kid

MAXINE WOLCOTT KLAN

Spina bifida didn't usually stop my five-year-old grandson Jaden from keeping up with his brothers and sisters. But after surgery to loosen the muscles in his knees and ankles, both his legs were in casts. He had to sit in a wheelchair during our trip to the zoo.

I wheeled Jaden down a wood-chip path. A low rope ran along its edge, dividing us from the kangaroos lazing in the grass. "Can we pet them?" Jaden asked the zoo attendant who was passing by.

"Yes, they're very friendly," she said. "But you must stay on the path."

The children rushed to the rope and stretched over it so they could pet those adorable creatures. Jaden reached for a kangaroo from his wheelchair but couldn't get anywhere close. *Must everything be so hard for him, Lord?*

Right then a kangaroo rolled over and stood on its hind legs. One, two, three hops and it was over the rope. The kangaroo lay at Jaden's feet! I sat my grandson down next to it. Jaden gently petted the animal between the ears.

The other children all gathered round to meet the accommodating kangaroo. The one that God sent just for Jaden.

Tickets from Heaven

TOM ELLIOTT

Baseball *is* a tradition in my family. Some of my best memories growing up were the days my dad took my brother and me on the ninety-minute drive to San Francisco to see the San Francisco Giants play at Candlestick Park. We saw a lot of baseball history being made, like when Willie Mays and the Giants won the National League pennant in 1962.

When I had my first child, Zach, Paw—as Zach called him—had another youngster to school in all things baseball. Unfortunately, by the time Zach was old enough to go to games, Paw could no longer go. He had Alzheimer's and had to move into an assisted-living facility. Zach couldn't understand that Paw would never "get better" or why we only saw him in his "new home."

"Why don't we take Paw with us to a Giants game, Dad?" Zach asked one day as we drove home from a visit. He wouldn't understand a medical explanation; I barely could. The permanence of this disease seemed completely unfair, the situation painful. But I couldn't bear to dash Zach's dream. I just couldn't. "Maybe someday we'll all see a game together," I said. Maybe someday.

Even if we couldn't attend ball games together, our bond of three generations stood strong. Paw was Zach's biggest fan until he passed away. After he died the world seemed pretty gray for all of us, but especially for Zach. "Now we'll never see that game together," Zach said the day of Dad's funeral. *I should never have raised Zach's hopes*, I thought. I always knew it couldn't happen.

Several weeks after Paw died, a good friend who was related to a Giants player offered us some complimentary tickets. I hesitated. Since his death, even baseball had lost some of its flavor. On the other hand, maybe that's just what we needed. *It's what Dad would want us to do*, I thought.

After thinking it through, I accepted my friend's offer.

We drove to the game in high spirits. "I can't wait!" Zach said as we entered the stadium. Pleasant memories of my father swirled around my head. *I went to see the Giants when I was Zach's age with you, Dad*, I thought as we walked up to the will-call window.

"First and last name with some ID, please," the attendant said.

I slid my driver's license under the partition and ruffled Zach's hair. The attendant flipped through a stack of envelopes. She looked worried.

"I'm sorry," she said finally, "there aren't any tickets here for you."

"There must be some mistake," I said. She checked again and still came up empty. We backed away from the window in shock. The game was sold out, and I didn't have the money for scalped tickets. *Lord, I should have been straight with Zach.* We weren't ever going to see a game with Dad, nor did it look like Zach and I would see this one.

Zach looked down at the ground upset, when someone walked over to us.

"Are you taking your young son to the game?" a kindly old gentleman asked.

"I was planning on it," I said, "but there was some sort of mix-up with our tickets. We didn't have any."

The man held up two. "Here," he said. "Why don't you take these?"

I blinked. Was he kidding? People didn't just give away tickets to sold-out games. "I'm sorry," I said. "I don't have the money for scalped tickets."

The man shook his head and waved the tickets at me. "Take them," he said. "I want your boy to see the game."

He put the tickets in my hand and walked off with a smile. I stared after him, still confused. "Thanks!" Zach hollered as the man disappeared into the sea of sports fans milling around the entrance. Zach tugged at my hand. "Come on, Dad. Let's go!"

Inside the stadium I led Zach toward the "nose bleeds," assuming we were seated up there. But when I looked at the box and seat numbers I stopped short and my mouth fell open. Zach bumped into me from behind.

"What's the matter, Dad?"

"These seats are right behind home plate," I said. "Only a few rows up!"

"Unbelievable," I muttered to myself all the way down to the seats. The seat next to us was empty. "The man who gave us the tickets must be coming," Zach said. "We can buy him a hot dog!"

It was one of the best games I ever saw. The Giants came back late with a grand slam to tie it up. They won in the bottom of the ninth with a slide around the tag at home plate. Zach and I were exhausted from hooting and hollering. When it was over I took a good hard look at the empty seat next to us.

"I can't believe nobody ever sat there," I said. "What a waste of a good seat."

"But, Dad," Zach said, "someone was sitting in the seat next to us."

Wow, could I really have been that caught up in the game?

"I didn't see a soul. Who was it?"

Zach grinned. "It was Paw, Dad. He was sitting right here with us the whole time. We finally did get to see that Giants game, the three of us."

I pulled Zach close. People around us must've thought we were feeling very emotional about the Giants' win. But only the two of us knew the truth: We were living a gift from above. Well, maybe three of us knew it. "Maybe that old man had it all planned all along," I said as we were leaving the stadium.

"I think that angel flew back up to heaven with Paw," said Zach. "They're probably rehashing the game." Just like Zach and I did all the way home.

Trouble on the Tracks

ONA DEANE

When I was a little girl in Buchanan, Virginia, seemed everyone in my family had something to do with trains. The men were railroad workers, and my great aunts ran rooming houses where the workers stayed. My whole family was crazy about trains. Except me. I was scared to death.

Still, I loved to spend time with my great-aunt Ren and great-uncle George, even if they did live right across the street from the railroad tracks. They had a big old house, a yard with two giant shade trees and a white picket fence.

My relatives liked to gather on their porch, tell stories, drink sweet tea and watch the trains go by. The roar of the engines always made me cry. Mother would run to my side and hold her hands over my ears till the offending train passed.

Uncle George took me for walks on the tracks. "Tooty," he said one day—everyone called me that back then—"you've got to keep your eye on the signal light down there." He pointed. I squinted and peered as far down as I could. "When it turns green, you've got to get off the tracks. Means a train is coming."

My family moved to Baltimore when I was eight, and those lazy afternoons on the porch ended. But then in the summer of 1946 I went back to Buchanan to visit.

"Let's take a walk," Cousin Jean said. She was twelve, I was thirteen. We set out, and before I knew it we were heading down a railroad track. I tried to stay calm, but I hadn't outgrown my fear.

I thought about Uncle George and tried to catch a glimpse of the signal light—but there was no light to be seen. Even worse, a stretch of the track was up on a trestle so there was nowhere to jump in case of danger—just briar patches on both sides, which I knew were full of snakes and other creepy crawlers.

I was so relieved when we made it to the end of that part of the track. Trouble was, we'd have to head back the same way.

Halfway down the trestle I heard a train coming. I glanced back and it was barreling down the track. "Hurry, Tooty!" Jean called out. "Run!"

I followed as fast as I could. Jean managed to jump off the trestle into a yard, but I couldn't catch up. The train was right up close to me. I froze.

Suddenly I felt a firm hand on my shoulder and a strong, comforting voice said, "Just stand still now, child."

I looked to my left, and there stood a man wearing a cap and bib overalls. A railroad worker! My fear ebbed away, even though if I stretched out my arm I could have touched the train. That's how close I was to it. I felt the engine's heat around my legs. The wind in the train's wake was so strong it could've sucked me under the wheels or off the trestle. But all this time the stranger held me in his gaze and kept me safe.

Just as quickly as the train came, it vanished—and so did the angel of a railroad worker. But where? There was nowhere for him to go. He just disappeared. It took me years before I realized that God had sent me a real angel that day. An angel dressed in railroad clothes so I'd feel as safe and secure as I did with the relatives I loved who proudly wore the same uniform.

10

ENSURING LIVELIHOOD

The history of [God's] wonders in the past is a constant succession
of new things, and he is not at the end of his resources yet.
—LILIAS TROTTER, *A Blossom in the Desert*

God is not at the end of his resources. That's what the writers in this section learned from the messengers who led them toward new jobs or stepped into their work environments to protect them—and their livelihood. These stories illustrate how God cares about all aspects of our lives. Although he does not open every door, we can be assured that the One who owns "the cattle on a thousand hills" (Psalm 50:10 NKJV) knows our needs—and is able to supply.

Messenger from the Sky

ROSE T. ZEILMAN

One August evening in 1980 I stood in my front yard, silent with wonder as streaks of silvery light shot across the sky. It was the time of the annual Perseid meteor showers, and the heavens were putting on a spectacular show. "It's great being here to see this, Mom," George said, putting his arm around my waist.

My son and his family had been living with me since spring. After eight years with a security job in the Air Force, he'd decided not to reenlist. He had packed everything in his Chevy truck and come home to Florida to start over as a civilian. "It'll be easier on my family," he said, and I agreed. George's father had been a career Navy man, and I worked at the Naval Air Station Jacksonville. I understood how difficult the military could be.

At first it was fun, all of us being together. The children were both only preschool age then and always wide-eyed with discovery. We took trips to St. Augustine and other Florida sights. We shared the chores and the baby-sitting, and my daughter-in-law Penney and I kept a jigsaw puzzle going on a table in the living room. We had cookouts in the backyard—hot dogs, sweet corn, watermelon and all the trimmings. But my house was small, and I'd been used to living alone. Spring had turned into summer, and the strain was beginning to show. George's job search had taken much longer than he'd expected, and he was beginning to become filled with self-doubt. Money was tight, and getting a job, any job, became critical.

That hot August night, as the celestial rockets plunged through the sky, I said a prayer for my son, asking God for some of that heavenly power to be directed to him and his need for work.

George slipped away at one point, and I noticed him down the street talking to someone. Their conversation seemed animated, and after a few minutes they shook hands. George started back home and then turned to wave. "Thanks, Jim!"

George hurried to me. "I have a job lead!" he said. He told me the man had recently moved from Merritt Island, home of the Kennedy Space Center. "Jim said they hire civilians for security jobs, and I'm qualified." There was a look of hope on my son's face I hadn't seen for months. "I'm going to drive down there," he said, "first thing in the morning."

"But you have no appointment," I said, "and no clearance. You just can't walk into a place like the Space Center." I was afraid my son was grasping at straws.

"I've a good feeling about this, Mom," George said. "I believe Jim knew what he was talking about. Wait and see."

By 6:30 the next morning George was in his Chevy truck, headed for Merritt Island. He came home that evening, triumphant. "I did it!" he said. "I'm hired!" It seemed like no less than a miracle. "I talked like I've never talked before," George explained. "I mentioned Jim, even though I didn't know his full name. I told them about the Air

Force and my family and how ready I was to go to work." He stopped to catch his breath. "I guess I just talked my way inside. They gave me a guest badge, and I was directed to personnel."

In ten days George found a place for his family to live on Merritt Island, and he started his job at the Space Center. The heavens had truly been filled with power that August night. An angel named Jim arrived on a meteor.

Our Best Customers Ever

MARILYN CALLALY

I leaned against the cooler in the downtown flower shop I ran with my husband, Hugh. Every bit of me ached. Working thirteen hours a day for a week straight has that effect on you, especially when you're coming up on sixty-five years old. But I had to do it. After all, the week leading up to Christmas was one of our busiest.

I glanced at the mirror and laughed. My Santa hat and poinsettia-print shirt were covered with gold and silver glitter. I looked a sight.

Outside, the late December sun cast a glow on the festive decorations. It was about four o'clock in the afternoon on Christmas Eve 1993. The rush was over and our floral designers were gone. The streets were deserted. Even the Salvation Army trio had packed up their instruments and gone home. Nothing to do now but lock the door, clean up the store and make sure all our holiday orders had been delivered.

Hugh picked up some flower buckets and dumped the water into the sink. "Another holiday down the drain," he said. He'd told the same joke every holiday for the past thirty-five years. Still, I laughed. It was a tradition.

Hugh went to straighten up in the back room and I grabbed a broom. As I circled the arranger's bench and neared the counter, my eye caught movement outside the front door. Next thing I knew the door flew open and three very large young men walked in. Hugh and I had run this shop for so long we knew everyone in town. Everyone and their guardian angels too. I had no clue who these three were. From the look of them, they were trouble. Grimy black leather jackets and filthy jeans. Wool caps pulled down low. Mean-looking. Real mean. I thought of what Hugh always told me: "If we are ever robbed, don't argue. Just do what you're told and give them whatever they want."

Lord only knew what they wanted. "Help you?" I managed to choke out.

They looked around and must have figured I was alone. They surrounded me. One of them blocked the door. The biggest thug flashed a cruel grin. "Hey, mama," he sneered. "Got any specials?" The other two snorted.

"I'm sorry," I said. "We're closed. I was just cleaning up."

"Whadda ya mean, closed?" he snapped. He brought his face right up to mine. "It's Christmas," he said. "I need some flowers. Now!"

His breath reeked. I turned my head, nearly gagging. I saw Hugh coming from the back room. He stopped short, took in the situation and then quickly came to my side. "What do you need, fellas?" Hugh said. "Make it quick."

"Lookie here, another one," said the leader. "You're not closing yet. First I wanna see what you got." He looked around. "Let's see them shiny things up there." He pointed toward the vase-filled shelves high on the wall. "Come on, let's see 'em."

Hugh reached to get one down.

"Not that one. The one over there." He pointed to the far end of the shelf and cackled. Hugh walked over and had just started to take the vase down when the thug said, "Old man, can't you get anything right? I meant the red one, back there." This time he pointed to another shelf.

The other two stood close by me. No way they'd let me make it to the phone, let alone the front door. The sun was down now. It was completely black. *Please, God, show us a way out of this.*

Hugh raced around the store, the three toying with him. They laughed harder and harder. Hugh got winded, disoriented. It seemed to go on forever. Suddenly Hugh stopped and shouted, "Enough! I've had enough!"

No, Hugh! Just do what they say.

"What do you mean 'enough,' old man?" the leader shouted. "We're just startin' to have fun, aren't we?" Suddenly all three converged on my husband. I ran to the phone.

At that moment the front door opened. A rush of cold winter air blew in. The thugs looked up. Two young men entered the shop. Both were neatly dressed in brown suits and hats. Each carried a briefcase. One of them walked over to the near-empty display case. The second walked up to the counter. Neither of them said a word.

In the silence, I felt a presence. My eardrums pounded from the overwhelming presence of strength and goodness. I glanced over at Hugh, untouched by the thugs. They seemed spellbound, frozen in mid-attack. They couldn't seem to take their eyes off the two mysterious young men.

Then I saw Hugh react, as if some power had struck him. He puffed up before my eyes. "You guys don't want anything," he yelled. "Quit jerking me around and get out of here!"

The thugs looked at Hugh and then at the two newcomers, who stared silently back. The tables had been turned. The menace in the hoodlums' eyes vanished and was replaced by fear. By sheer terror! They bolted for the door and disappeared back into the night.

I tried to collect myself, thanking our two saviors again and again. They didn't look identical, yet I could not help but think of them as twins.

"Do you have a white rose?" one asked. "Do you have a white rose?" repeated the other.

"I'm so sorry, no," I said. "Could I offer you a red one instead?"

They shook their heads no, said thank you and turned to leave.

Hugh followed them to the door, locked it behind them and then switched off the overhead lights. He reached out to me and I hugged him close, still trembling. It was a long time till I finally broke the silence. "Those young men . . ."

"Never saw them before in my life."

We knew everyone in town, all right, but it appeared that there were a few guardian angels we hadn't yet met.

Hide nor Hair

MARINE WOLF

A rancher like me knows his cows, and his cows know him. They're kind of like dogs. Mine recognize my voice or the sound of the horn on my pickup, and they amble toward me, good as gold. Naturally, they'll trot up even faster if I have a bucketful of grain. I'd swear they could spot that bucket a mile away. But just the toot of my horn will always get their attention. They know food will be their reward.

One March day, I'd turned the cattle into my north field. In total I had about twenty cows and two calves. It would soon be time to disk the ground for a new summer crop, and I wanted them to find anything green they could eat.

Toward evening I drove over to my north fence and tooted on my horn. I waited and waited. Nobody came. So I drove out into the field looking for them. As the saying goes, there wasn't hide nor hair of cows or calves.

"Where have you gone?" I asked, calling into the wind. I waited some more. Nothing. They hadn't heard my horn or my voice.

I got worried. There were rustlers in Kansas who'd steal your cattle. I got out of my pickup and walked the north fence that divided my land from my neighbor's. Then I saw trouble, a spot where the barbed-wire fence was down. My cows had gone through there for sure. I tooted on my horn again. No response, and no sight of my cattle. "What am I supposed to do now, Lord?" I said.

I headed back to the house for a bucket of grain, meaning to drive around on the roads in hopes I'd see some trace of my cows. A pickup pulled into my yard with a cattle trailer behind it. A man leaned out the window. "Missing some cows?" he said.

"You bet."

"I know where they are. Grazing in a wheat field to the northeast," the man said, getting out of his truck. "I'm sure they'll follow that bucket of grain." I'd never seen this man before, but he sure seemed to know my cows.

I jumped back in the driver's seat. "Got some free time," the man said and climbed into my pickup with me. I nodded in appreciation. Ranchers don't talk much. Helping a neighbor in need does the talking for us. We drove back to the downed fence.

"Your cows are beyond that windbreak over there," the man said. I grabbed the bucket of grain and we set off. Tall rows of red cedars surrounded a dense wilderness of deciduous trees. It was rough going. Branches whipped at our faces and slashed our shins. The ground was covered with deadfall trees and rocks.

We came to a large creek. How that man got across the water, I'll never know. I sure didn't see him do it. I had to crawl over on a dead tree lying from one bank to the other, all the while trying to balance my bucket of grain and not fall into the creek. After that it was a steep uphill climb to the wheat field.

"My cows!" I cried. "There they are!" They grazed on the other side of a barbed-wire fence, and the man and I crawled over it. The cows had heard my voice and hurried toward me when they saw the bucket. They followed me, but when they got to the fence, they couldn't go any farther. "I know how they got out of my fence," I said, "but how did they get in this one?"

The man shook his head. "It would take a lot of walking to figure out where your cattle found another hole," he said. "My horse and dog are in my trailer. I'll get those cattle to you."

We made our way back to my pickup and drove to my house. The man led his horse from the trailer and mounted up, with his dog yipping close behind, eager to come along. "Give me twenty minutes," he said. "I'll ride around to that wheat field and get behind the cows. Go back to the hole in your fence and honk your horn."

This I dutifully did. Before I knew it, my cattle came. Right behind them was a dog and this man on his horse. I stared at him in wonder. It was all we could do to get ourselves through that wilderness on foot. How could he have done it on horseback?

I looked at the man and mustered up my courage to speak. "Do you believe in angels?" I asked.

"As a matter of fact I do," he said. The man laughed. It was a hearty, sincere kind of laugh, like he was enjoying himself. "I know what you're thinking," he said. "But if I'm one of your guardian angels, maybe I should be just a little bit angry. God sure made me do a lot of work!"

Then the man pulled the reins, and with a wave he was off, his dog yipping close behind him. His job was done.

My cows followed me back home. When I returned, the man's pickup and trailer were gone from my yard, but I would never forget him. Who had helped me, a man or an angel? Whoever he was, I've not seen hide nor hair of him since.

Lost and Found

JEFFREY MORGAN

I have an early morning job driving a produce delivery truck. Before my shift even starts, I drive twenty miles to New Jersey, where I park my car and pick up my truck. From there I unlock the sliding cargo door, put my delivery keys on the rear ledge, and hop on the tailgate to check every customer's order to make sure it is complete and lined up correctly. My customers rely on my efficiency. A mistake on my part could seriously compromise their menus, so I had their backs when it came to reliability.

One morning I was making my way through Connecticut to my first stop at a country club. I backed my truck up to the loading dock and said my hellos to the kitchen staff. I walked toward the back of the truck, reaching my hand into my pocket to fish out the delivery keys. My pocket was empty. I'd left the keys on the tailgate back in Jersey! How would I make my deliveries?

Rounding the back of the truck I stopped short. A smile crept across my face. *The keys!* They were sitting on the tailgate exactly where I'd left them, not hung or caught on anything, just resting right on the rear ledge of the truck. How they stayed there over the course of fifty highway miles, I'll never know. What I do know is my delivery truck angel had my back that morning.

Bottom of the Ninth

BRUCE RICE

I love baseball cards and I love collecting them. I've loved them all my life, just like my dad. But that autumn day twelve years ago was different. I'd come to work early at my sports cards-and-collectibles shop. Owning the store had been a dream come true. But I'd purchased thousands of baseball cards in anticipation of a big summer sale and, just as they arrived, major-league baseball went on strike. The World Series was canceled. Kids turned away from the game. My sales dove.

I stared at the walls, countertops, display cases—all of them filled with my beloved vintage cards. *Lord,* I wondered, *why did I go into this business? Wasn't this what I thought you were blessing?*

I'd been a successful shoe-store manager for twenty years. I put in long hours, but I was happy to continue at it the rest of my career. I'd never thought of a job in sports memorabilia. To me, baseball was a passion, something to share with my children. At night I'd pull out a box of cards, sit on the floor with my three kids and tell them stories about favorite players and old nemeses, the way other dads shared bedtime stories. "That's Bill Mazeroski, second baseman for the Pittsburgh Pirates," I'd say. "In 1960 he hit the home run that beat the Yankees in the World Series." I'd grin and then add, "The rat."

Our life in San Antonio was wonderful. My wife, Debbie, and I loved our community and our church. I made a good living in the shoe business. Now and then I'd visit a collectibles shop and buy a Cal Ripken, Ozzie Smith or Roger Clemens card for the kids—players I thought might one day win election to the Hall of Fame. I was content, blessed.

In 1993 the roof fell in. Management at work changed. I was laid off. Debbie was worried. "We need your income," she said.

I'd seldom been out of a job before. But I saw this as an opportunity. I started looking for a shoe store I could purchase. Then, one day, a business associate approached. "Hey, I know you're looking to buy a business," he said. "Well, there's a San Antonio sports-card shop for sale."

I raced home. "What do you think, Debbie? This is the best chance we'll ever have to buy our own business," I said. "Something the whole family can share in. It'll give me more time with the kids."

We thought and prayed about it for a week, and then agreed. "I know this is your dream," Debbie said.

We bought the place and spruced it up. Slowly but surely, collectors came in. And not just baseball fans. I carried stuff from every major sport.

I spent most of our revenue on new inventory—the sports cards and autographed memorabilia. I anticipated that 1994 would be a big year for baseball, and I wanted to be ready, so I invested heavily in the baseball side of things.

That spring, we started out like gangbusters. Players were slugging home runs left and right. San Diego Padres outfielder Tony Gwynn seemed on target to become the first player to bat .400 for a season since Ted Williams last did it, in 1941. "Debbie," I said, "I'm going to sink every penny we can into buying inventory. We have to strike while the iron's hot."

The card shipments arrived in August. The pennant race was heating up, the home-run hitters kept slugging, Gwynn's batting average hovered around .400. "We're going to have a great two months," I told Debbie. "This will push us over the top."

If only I'd known. Days later the baseball players went on strike and, for the first time ever, the baseball commissioner canceled the World Series. Sales stopped cold. We went from selling three hundred dollars' worth of baseball cards a day to five dollars' worth. We burned through our business account and then through our personal account.

After one particularly bad Saturday, Debbie totaled up our meager sales for the day and began to cry. "Honey, we're going to go bankrupt," she said. "We're going to lose everything."

I put on a strong face, but inside I was as frightened as she. *We're down to one hundred dollars in our checking account. What happens if the roof leaks or the car needs a major repair? How will we pay for it?*

The next morning our refrigerator broke. The repairman said it would cost two hundred dollars to fix. So on that baseball-less autumn day, I went to the store early. I needed to think. I looked around at my beloved cards, thousands of them, and collapsed into a chair by the counter. *Lord,* I begged, *I can't pay for the refrigerator. I can't provide for my family. I don't know if I should sell the store or try to see this through. Please show me a sign. Something. Anything.*

The phone rang. It was a stranger on the line. "Do you have Troy Aikman's rookie card?" she asked. Aikman was the Dallas Cowboys' star quarterback. His rookie card was worth a pretty penny.

"Sure do," I said.

"How about Emmitt Smith's rookie card?" Smith, too, was then a Cowboys star.

"Yes, ma'am, I have it," I responded.

She told me she would be right over.

Half an hour later a well-dressed woman and her teenaged son breezed through the door. "Let me see those Aikman and Smith rookie cards, please," she said. Then the two of them started opening boxes of football cards, going through them like kids at a carnival. They whooped and laughed, pointing out this player and that. I mean, they carried on quite a bit. It seemed almost unreal.

The woman handed me a credit card. "Bill me five hundred dollars and tell me when we've used it up," she said. She and her son turned their attention back to the cards. Looking at the fun they were having, at the bond they shared, reminded me of myself and my dad—of myself and my own kids. I remembered why I'd purchased the business in the first place: to have more time with my family. *Lord, thanks for reminding me.*

The woman bought seven hundred dollars' worth of cards! After she left, I figured out my profit: two hundred and one dollars, one dollar more than the bill for the refrigerator. That dollar meant as much to me as a million. It was a sign. I called Debbie. "Pay the bill. We have the money. We're going to be okay."

Twelve years have passed. We're still in business and we're doing well. Debbie and I raised our kids as much in the store as we did at home. It was like our second living room.

One day my kids asked me about the strange lady. She's become a bit of a legend in our family, like one of those old baseball heroes on my vintage cards. I told them the story again. "I think about her every day," I said. "I only wish I could thank her. She came into our lives when we needed her most, and I've never heard from or seen her again."

Paperboy Angel

BARBARA SHOEMAKER

One night my husband, Don, stepped around the pile of newspapers on our porch and came in the door looking troubled. "I'm worried," he said, "about my job at the Katy." That was our nickname for the M-K-T, the Missouri, Kansas and Texas Railroad. Jobs were scarce in our small town of Parsons, Kansas, in the 1950s. Any position at the Katy was prime. Don was an IBM tab operator, an early form of data processing. His job was one of the best.

The Katy had been good to us. I met Don there on my first day of work, and we got married ten months later. Steady work and good pay meant Don and I could afford a cozy first-floor apartment in an old two-story house. I was even able to stay home after I had our first baby. It seemed like we were settled for life. But that night Don was concerned about our future. "Change is in the air. I can tell," he said.

"God will handle it," I said. "Whatever it is."

Next morning I noticed yet another newspaper on top of the pile on our porch. I'd figured they belonged to our landlady, who lived upstairs.

"They're not mine," she said. "I thought they were yours."

Before I threw the papers away, I glanced at one. *The Tulsa World*. Tulsa, Oklahoma, was about 125 miles south of us. What were these papers doing here on our front porch? No sense letting all this information go to waste, I figured. I put them aside to share with Don.

"Something's definitely up at the Katy," Don told me one night. "I'm afraid I may lose my job."

"What will we do?" I asked.

"I'll just have to look around," Don said. "The Katy isn't the whole world."

World? I thought of the newspapers I'd saved. "Maybe you could find something here," I said. I gave him the stack.

"Guess what," Don said as he looked over the employment ads. "There are openings for tab operators in Tulsa."

The *World* arrived on our doorstep Monday through Friday. Each evening Don read the employment ads, and the papers piled up by his chair just as they had on the porch. "Looks like there are plenty of good jobs," he said. "We should investigate." It was hard to accept the idea of life away from Parsons, but maybe that's what God had in mind.

We drove to Tulsa on Sunday afternoon, checked into a hotel and picked up a weekend edition of the *World*. Inside was a large help-wanted ad for an IBM tab operator at American Airlines. "Say a prayer, honey," Don told me. "I'm going to be there the second the office opens tomorrow morning."

Don was first in line. By noon he had a new job. We found a place to live. Don went back to the Katy the following morning to give his notice. "Sorry to lose you," his boss said, "but your timing is good. Things are changing here."

The Tulsa World didn't appear on our porch that day or any other day before we moved away. Our life, which had seemed so settled, took quite a turn. Don retired in 1991, after thirty-six years with American Airlines. We still live in Tulsa, and the *World* is delivered to our home every day. We're subscribers now. We've known all our paperboys by name. Except, of course, that one.

11

ALTERING PATHS

We encounter God in new places: in the cyclone, in the dark,
in the crisis that shatters our old confining consciousness.
It is this severity that makes us new.
—SUE MONK KIDD, *Firstlight*

A wake-up call. That's the phrase we often use to refer to an event that turns us around, from apathy to action, from addiction to sobriety, from near-death to Life. Though some wake-up calls can be traumatic, when we view them through a lens of grace, we can be overwhelmed with gratitude that we've been set on a new path. Sometimes by angels sent on a transformative mission.

"Do You Want to Live?"

MICHAEL P. KELLY

On a beautiful morning in September 1988, I was at home, slouched in my favorite wicker captain's chair, reading the local paper and sipping a can of beer. I'd picked up the paper with the thought of perusing the Help Wanted section but was distracted by an article on the front page about the launch of the space shuttle Discovery the next day. Through the haze of my usual hangover, an idea popped into my head. I still had a little cash from the last job I'd quit. Why not hitchhike down to Cape Canaveral, spend the night under the stars and watch the shuttle launch in person?

Crazy last-minute adventures were a favorite pastime of mine. After all, the way I saw it, the basic purpose of life was to have a good time. Nothing else much mattered. By noon I was on the side of the highway with a blanket, a cooler and a big cardboard sign that said simply: LAUNCH.

A couple of hours later I found myself at the Titusville Causeway exit of I-95, right next to Cape Canaveral. People from all over the state and beyond had set up campsites, and tailgate picnics were in full swing. I found a clear spot and spread out my bedroll. Off in the distance, the Kennedy Space Center looked like a picture on a postcard. Everything was perfect.

Well, almost perfect. A six-pack or two would be nice. Maybe I could catch a quick ride to a convenience store.

I didn't have long to wait. A big black pickup with three young men in the cab pulled over.

"Where you headed?"

"To get some beer."

"Hop on."

I clambered onto the back and we rumbled off. *Typical rednecks,* I thought as I took in the three grimy, tousled heads in the cab in front of me and the big rifle rack above them. They'd probably just got off work and were ready to cop a buzz. I guessed we had that in common.

We pulled up in front of a convenience store and I handed one of the guys a couple of bucks. The three of them went in, leaving me in the back of the truck. There was definitely something off about these guys—but they were getting beer, and that was what counted. Even after they pulled back out onto the highway in the opposite direction from the launch site I didn't really worry about it. *They must know a good place to party,* I figured.

After a mile or so the driver turned down a narrow dirt road that led through dense woods. We pulled up at a small clearing overlooking a drainage canal that meandered through the trees. One of the guys tossed me a beer and I cracked it. They still didn't look any too savory, with their scraggly hair and tobacco-stained teeth, but they were friendly enough.

Then out of nowhere, one of them reached into the truck and grabbed a rifle off the rack. "Gimme your money," he growled, poking me in the belly with the barrel, "and pull those pants down."

"Hey, c'mon. We were just . . ."

"Shut up and do it now, dummy, less you want to get shot!"

Terror and humiliation were sobering me up fast. Hands trembling, I handed over my last five and lowered my pants. He kept the gun trained on me.

Then he pulled the trigger.

I collapsed onto the ground, doubled up in agony. Waves of pain radiated out of my groin. Whooping, the men kicked at my legs and back, edging me forward. The ground dropped away, and I splashed into the canal. When my head cleared the water, I caught a glimpse of the darkening sky directly above me. Then I saw the silhouettes of the three men on the bank. "This one's for the road," one of them shouted. There was a dull pop, and a skewer of pain shot through my abdomen.

Make this stop, I found myself silently pleading—to whom or what, I didn't know. *Please just make all of this stop.*

"Do you want to live?"

The words sounded clearly in my ears. But who had spoken?

Yes, yes, I want to live!

"Then you must get out of the water."

The words were like a wake-up call, snapping me into action. I paddled to the far shore and struggled up the steep, muddy bank. I reached the top, only to slide back down into the water. I tried a second time and then a third. The pain in my gut was wrenching. But I knew I had to get up that bank or die trying. With everything I had, I lunged for the top one more time.

I made it. "Hide." The voice was calm, clear and firm, just as it had been before. Frantically looking around, I spotted a mass of thick underbrush. I plunged in, trying to sink down out of sight. As I did so, headlights appeared on the other side of the drainage ditch. The voice was right. *They're looking for me! They must want to make sure they finished me off.* I lay face down, absolutely motionless, listening to the men's angry shouts as they slogged back and forth along the bank with a flashlight.

After a few minutes I heard the truck engine start up again, then gradually fade in the distance. My tormentors were gone. With a heave I flipped myself onto my back. The movement sent pain blazing through my gut. I groaned involuntarily and then lay still.

The less I moved, the less I hurt. I closed my eyes. When I opened them again it was completely dark. I sensed immediately that I was not alone. Something—a presence of some kind—was there with me in the darkness. And I just knew it was the same presence that had spoken to me in the water earlier. I felt it focusing on me now, filling me up with an indescribable sense of peace and ease. Dehydrated, exhausted, bleeding from the gunshot wounds, I nonetheless began to feel shielded from my body's pain.

A new presence appeared—not a single one this time, but a group—male and female, old and young, all dressed in different colors, like peasants from some faraway time and place. Slowly they began to reach out to me. Their faces were clear despite the darkness. Who they were or where they came from I had no idea, but under their healing touch, the pain and the fear receded. No one spoke, yet I had a sensation of total gentleness and peace, beyond anything I had ever felt or imagined.

All through the night the visitations continued. Soon even the trees and the grass around me began to carry the same glow of peace that emanated from them. I could feel it washing through me, penetrating every cell in my body. Consciousness came and went like a tide.

Finally dawn arrived, and the visitations slowly faded. In the early morning silence, I could make out the sound of cars in the near distance. I crawled to a tree and pulled myself to my feet. Letting go for a second to get my pants up, I immediately fell back onto the ground, pain once again racking my stomach and groin.

The voice from the previous evening returned, clear as ever. "If you can't walk, crawl."

Lying on my back, I wriggled and pulled until my pants were up. Every movement was agony now. Inch by painful inch, I crawled toward the sound of the traffic. Just as before, the voice filled me with inner determination. *I'm going to make it out of here.*

I'd almost made it to the road when a man walking with his son stumbled across me. They ran for help, and in half an hour I was at a hospital. A CAT scan revealed that the second bullet had ruptured my bladder and lodged in my right hip. "I don't believe it," the doctor who performed the operation told me later. "A single nick in your intestine, and you would have died during the night."

The first bullet ended up leaving surprisingly minimal damage as well. One of the doctors suggested that because it had been fired at such close range, it had actually cauterized the wound as it passed through my body.

Lucky or not, I can't say I wasn't angry after my ordeal. Yet even though they were never brought to justice, I began to pray for the men who almost killed me. I pray that God will reach them, just as he finally reached me.

I've come to realize that even the most painful and ugly things that happen in life can ultimately have a positive outcome. Before my ordeal I was basically a person adrift— someone who moved from day to day alone, ruled only by my own personal whims. Nowadays I think about a whole lot more than where the next bit of fun is coming from. And it's definitely not in a six-pack of beer. God has given me a role to play in the world, and it's up to me to find out, each and every day, what I need to do to fulfill it.

The voice that came to me that terrible day ended up doing more than just rescuing me from death. It rescued me from the person I had been, showing me that another, better, truer one had been inside me all along, just waiting to get out.

Happy Again

CONSTANCE KIRK

*S*unshine burst through the tall glass windows and the first light notes of the "Appalachia Waltz" sounded from the string trio. I took a deep breath, squeezed my bridal bouquet of white calla lilies and started my slow procession down the aisle. How happy I felt in this moment, happier than I'd ever dreamed possible. Ken, my groom, took my arm and we approached the altar. My best friend stood beside me as my honor attendant. Her bouquet of pink calla lilies was perfect, the sturdy, cylindrical petals peeking out from a spray of baby's breath. *Like spongy pink hair curlers,* I thought. Hair curlers. Not the most romantic comparison but one that had special significance to me. In a way it was curlers that had gotten me here today.

Seven years ago, I'd taken a short trip away from my home in New York City. It had been ages since I'd spent the night alone in a hotel. Just divorced at thirty-four, I'd forgotten how to enjoy anything on my own. A favorite restaurant, an afternoon movie, even the church my husband and I had attended every Sunday all seemed strange without him, and I ended up staying at home more and more. I lay on top of the thin hotel bedspread, staring up at the stucco ceiling. The television droned in the background. *Will I ever get used to this?*

I woke up in the same position at 3:00 AM. The hotel fire alarm was going off. Quick as I could I pulled on a robe, grabbed my room key and joined the other guests filing into the parking lot. I stared at the ground, running a bare toe over the gravel while firemen checked out the problem. The other guests huddled together in their pajamas. A flash of pink caught my eye, and I stepped forward to see what it was. The crowd parted around me to reveal a little lady in a terrycloth bathrobe and slippers. Her gray hair was completely rolled in dozens of pale-pink curlers, and she held her robe tight to her neck. *She's all alone, like me,* I thought. *I wonder if she's scared.* I stood beside her, as much for her comfort as for mine.

"What brings you here?" the woman turned and asked.

I looked into her face. She seemed to be in her seventies, but her twinkling eyes belied her age. "I needed to get away," I said. "I recently divorced, and the future seems so uncertain." *Had I just said that to a complete stranger?*

The woman put her hand on my arm and shook her head, making the curlers bounce. "Oh, you mustn't think like that," she said. She leaned in close. I bent down to listen, bumping my nose on a spongy pink curler. "Keep the faith," she whispered in my ear. "The best is yet to come." Could that really be true? Looking into the woman's sparkling eyes, I couldn't help but think that maybe, just maybe, it could be.

"False alarm," the hotel manager called out. "We apologize for the inconvenience." I held out my arm to escort the woman back into the hotel, but she was no longer standing beside me. I scanned the crowd for the head full of pink curlers. *Strange,* I thought. *Not just her disappearance, but the warm, hopeful feeling in my chest.*

I took the feeling back home with me, determined to make a new life for myself. The first time I entered a restaurant alone, I wanted to run right out the door before I even looked at the menu. I forced myself to stay. And traveling filled me with dread no matter where I was going. "This just isn't working," I sighed one evening after returning home early from a weekend at the beach. "I just can't hack it alone." But before I could throw out my suitcases, I heard the voice of the lady in pink curlers: "Keep the faith. The best is yet to come."

Keep the faith. Had I really been doing that? I hadn't been to church since my divorce. *It's time to give it a try,* I decided. After all, there were other churches in New York besides the one I'd belonged to with my husband. I just had to find the one that was right for me.

I started visiting churches, and my prayer was the same in each one: "God, I need your help finding my place in this world." It wasn't easy sitting in a pew by myself, but it wasn't impossible, either. Each Sunday was a small victory. I began to venture out on my own: movies, museums, bookshops. Eventually I decided to use my frequent flyer miles and take a weeklong solo trip to Paris. *The best is yet to come,* I reminded myself on the Champs-Élysées.

Upon my return, I resumed my Sunday research. I'd visited a dozen churches before I finally dropped in at St. Clement's, which I'd often walked past. The building left a lot to be desired, its red paint peeling, but I got a good feeling as soon as I sat down inside. The preacher had a way of speaking that drew me in and made me feel right at home. "Loving God is a process," he said. "It brings us out of isolation and into the embrace of a community."

I went back to St. Clement's the following Sunday and the next after that. In between I actually enjoyed my life, even the quiet times alone. In fact, I found myself scheduling time alone. I was happy again. Soon I wasn't waiting for Sunday to go to church. I volunteered for some of the outreach programs the church sponsored and got to know the preacher. We became quite good friends along the way. That friendship turned to love, and Ken asked me to marry him. I'd never been so sure of anything as I was about accepting his proposal.

The final notes of the string trio faded, and I turned to face Ken for our vows. I looked into his eyes as he slipped the wedding ring on my finger and thought about that little lady in the hotel parking lot, pink curlers bobbing in her hair. "The best is yet to come," she'd said and she was right. I had found happiness, on my own and with Ken. All I had to do was keep the faith. A faith that today Ken and I keep together.

Escape

WADIM KAMINSKY

*M*assive wooden doors slammed shut, sealing my doom. On a cold early dawn in 1946, I was on a train from the German town of Düren, on the way to my death. There was no escape.

I had grown up in a world at war. Fear loomed like a dark cloud over our beautiful Ukrainian city of Odessa. Under Stalin's rule anyone could be shot as an enemy of the state or sent to Siberia for hard labor. Boys had no choice but to be trained as soldiers in the Soviet Red Army, and we were taught that we were invincible. For a while, I believed it. But my father always said only God is invincible. In spite of the Soviet Union's official atheism, my family went to mass in secret, under cover of darkness. My heart pounded in fear. Would someone see us? Would Stalin find out? "Don't be afraid," my father would say. "God is with us."

I was in military school when Hitler's army invaded in 1941. At nineteen years old, I was given the rank of lieutenant and sent to fight the Nazis. I wept when I wasn't allowed to say good-bye to my parents, but no one dared question the regime.

One day in 1942 the Germans captured more than fifty thousand of us. I spent two years in prisoner-of-war camps, learning the hard lessons of war, erasing the lies we'd been taught in school. We were not invincible. Stalin was a monster who slaughtered his own people, and I feared my family was among them. If I survived, I vowed to fight for an end to Stalin and his power.

When World War II was over I went to Germany to join forces against Soviet communism. My decision tore me apart. Even if my parents were still alive, I couldn't return home. I'd be executed as a traitor. In a Germany divided into American, British, Soviet and French sectors, I gathered information for the American Counterintelligence Corps. But I couldn't escape Stalin's far-reaching tentacles.

One night an assignment took me into the British sector. I was on edge. My heart pounded with fear, just like those nights long ago when I sneaked through the streets of Odessa to go to mass with my parents. I was supposed to meet a man from counter-intelligence but was met by Russian soldiers instead. Someone had betrayed me.

At dawn I was taken to the railroad station in Düren. A guard in a gun turret kept watch on the roof of the train. I was thrown into a boxcar along with several other Russian soldiers who'd turned their backs on Stalin. Dim light filtered through the slats of the car. I scanned every nook and cranny of the inside of that boxcar, looking for an escape. None. Our fate was certain. I noticed a gray-haired man crouched on the floor in one corner. How had I missed him? He wore civilian clothes, and unlike the rest of us, he had a suitcase. Odd that he would have gotten it past the guards. I looked around at the other soldiers. It seemed we had all seen the mysterious man at the same time. We were all watching him, as if waiting for him to tell us what to do. The man didn't seem to be afraid. There was a feeling of calm about him, a strong sense of faith like my father's. I could almost hear the man speak: "Don't be afraid. God is with us."

"You can escape," the man said. *Escape? Impossible.* But the man opened his suitcase and pulled out a sharp-pointed tool. He dug at the floor of the boxcar, trying to cut a hole. The attempt failed. The wood was too thick and wet from the recent rains.

"Fools!" I said. "It's no use." The man gestured upward. "Try it," he said. A soldier boosted another up and held him as he hacked at the roof with the tool. Slowly an opening was made. I could see the morning fog and the smoke from the locomotive rushing by the hole in the roof!

Soon the hole was big enough for someone to slip through. I was sweating with anticipation. In spite of myself, I felt excitement. Maybe it was possible after all! When the train slowed to pass a station, soldiers boosted a comrade up and helped him climb out onto the roof and into the fog. From there he would jump to freedom. That was the plan.

"The guard will see him!" I said. "He'll be shot!" I held my breath. No gunshot was heard.

"He did it!" I exclaimed. We cheered. One by one, the soldiers boosted each other up and out onto the roof. There were no gunshots. All were free. *God is with us on this train,* I thought. *It was just the man and me.* "Now it's your turn," he said.

"But you—" I protested.

"No," the man said. "They won't harm me."

Without another word, his hands gripped my body, and he lifted me up. I crawled out onto the swaying roof. The fog was dense and cold. I lay as flat as I could to hide from the guard in the gun turret. Then I moved forward, inch by inch. Finally I reached the edge of the roof. The ground rushed by below. With a heave, I pushed myself away from the car and jumped.

I tumbled down a steep embankment, rocks cutting into my clothes. The train thundered by, its whistle wailing. Then it disappeared in the fog.

Nothing seemed real. The train. My escape. The mysterious man who had helped us get to freedom. I was never able to find my parents again, but I saw the end of Stalin's rule. And I live with the faith I learned despite him. God is invincible.

All Part of the Plan

EILEEN FANNING FISHER

*M*y sister and I shared a corned-beef sandwich at the Irish Heritage Festival in the park. "Do you want to join in the ceilidh dancing?" she asked.

"You go ahead, Mary. I'll watch."

Mary wove her way around some laughing children and took her place in the reel. I dreaded telling her my devastating news. I'd gotten my diagnosis the day before. Breast cancer.

Only my husband knew about it, and I'd made Scott promise not to tell anyone. I imagined the sadness in Mary's eyes when she found out. Worse yet, I could feel her fear. It would be the same with everyone I told: my parents, all of my friends—and my daughter Molly, only seven. How could I bear hurting the people I loved?

Mary rushed back to me, her cheeks flushed from dancing. I didn't have the heart to tell her my secret. I couldn't imagine that I ever would.

"I can't do it," I said to Scott once I got home. "I'm afraid and I can't worry everyone I care about."

Scott tried to reason with me, but it was no use. I had to face my illness alone.

That night I went to bed early. I dreamed I was surrounded by darkness so deep no light could reach it. And I was by myself, disconnected from everything that mattered. No love, no hope, no family. *No God.*

I woke with a start, trembling with the sense of overpowering loss. *That must be what hell is like.* I pulled the covers over my head and shut my eyes.

Sunday morning I sat up in bed and massaged my temples. My terrible dream still lingered in my thoughts. Scott was already dressed—in a suit, no less. "Where are you going?" I asked.

"I'm coming to church with you," he said. That was unusual for Scott, but I knew he was doing it for me.

Molly and I got dressed, and after breakfast we headed out to the late-morning service. The church I attended was some distance away, but I didn't mind the quiet morning drive through the wooded New Jersey countryside. I looked forward to sitting in the pew with my family around me. I wanted to feel God's reassuring presence. I wanted to forget all about that awful dream.

Going south on Route 23, we hit a roadblock. A police car was pulled across both lanes of the highway. Flashing lights signaled some trouble down the way. An officer motioned for us to turn around. He wouldn't tell us what the problem was. We had no choice.

"I don't know any other way to get there," I said. Scott turned the car around. "There must be another church around here," he said. "Let's look."

Up ahead a steeple rose above the treetops. "There!" I said. I read the sign as we got closer. Cars were just pulling in for the eleven o'clock service.

I'm here, Lord, I thought as we walked inside the church. *I need to know that you're with me.*

The service was pleasant enough, yet I struggled to feel God's reassurance. All through the sermon I couldn't shake the loneliness and despair from in my dream. If I couldn't face telling anyone about my cancer diagnosis, how was I going to face fighting the cancer itself?

We filed out with the congregation after the last hymn. "Eileen!" A woman I didn't recognize hurried toward me. "It's Meg Garrett! From the kids' camp, remember? We're starting a Bible study here in the annex on Tuesday mornings," she said. "Won't you come? We need some new members."

I was never any good at names, but I usually had a knack for remembering faces. I had absolutely no recollection of ever meeting this woman. Yet Molly *had* gone to day camp . . . "Can you make it?" Meg asked again.

Somehow I couldn't say no. "Sure," I said. "I'll try to make it."

"I don't know how she remembers me," I said to Scott on the way home. Perhaps she had mistaken me for another Eileen? No matter. I doubted I'd be going back to that church on Tuesday. What were the chances of our ever running into Meg again?

Come Monday night I couldn't get Meg off my mind. "I don't have anything else to do tomorrow," I told Scott as we got into bed. "The only things on my schedule for the next few months are doctor visits. Maybe a Bible study will help keep me focused."

The next morning I went back to the church. I parked my car in front of the annex. Women I didn't know chatted, pulling up folding chairs and drinking coffee. I took a seat and immediately regretted it. *What am I doing here?* No Bible study would solve this problem. I glanced at the door, wondering if I could slip out unnoticed.

A woman stood up. "We have three classes to choose from," she explained. I half-listened to the first two classes, and then she named the last one. "Lord Heal My Hurts," the woman announced. "God as the Great Physician."

I settled into my seat. This was the reassurance I'd craved.

"I'm glad you came," whispered Meg, sitting down beside me.

If only she knew! It had taken a mysterious roadblock, a late-morning church service and a friend I didn't remember to rescue me. But once God got hold of me, he didn't let me go. He helped me share the burden of my illness with my sister Mary and the rest of my family, and with my new friends at Bible study.

With everyone's loving support, I made it through chemotherapy and some difficult decisions about my treatment. Five years later, God is still with me. Fear is just a memory.

Better Things

LISA COBURN

igarette smoke hung in the air around me. The club door opened, letting in a breeze from the street. A customer stepped inside. Just another man in a dark suit and tie. Traveling on business, no doubt. Graying hair at his temples gave him a distinguished air, but surely he was the same as all the rest.

I leaned against the wall, avoiding the dirty mirror inches away. I didn't like to see myself dressed as an exotic dancer. Around the club, men sipped overpriced drinks, chatted up the girls, applauded the dancer onstage. I felt cold, familiar anger inside me—men were all the same. Any one of them would take advantage of me if he could. I'd learned that the hard way.

At seventeen, I'd accepted a ride home from college with an acquaintance. The drive turned into a nightmare when he forced himself on me. "Don't even think about telling anyone," he threatened. "I'll kill your family."

I didn't tell a soul. Not even my closest friends. I tried to go on with my life, but I felt like a fake. I looked like any normal student on the outside, but inside I felt dirty and worthless.

I dropped out of school. Friends and family were confused by my decision, so it seemed more important than ever to pretend I was the girl I always was. I dated a nice guy named Danny and thought I'd found my salvation when he proposed. I vowed to be the perfect wife. That would take away my shame.

But marriage didn't change a thing. *How long could I keep up this charade? I was only pretending to be a respectable wife. If my husband knew the truth about me, he would leave me in a heartbeat.* So I left him first.

A few months after Danny and I separated, I ran into an old classmate. "You won't believe what I'm doing," she said. "Exotic dancing at a gentlemen's club."

"How can you stand it?" I asked.

My friend shrugged. "It's no big deal. I dance in a skimpy outfit and flirt. The pay's not bad either," she said.

A place like that is where you belong, I told myself. *It's all you're good for.*

And there I was. Working in a club, hating myself as much as the men there. I kept my job a secret from Danny. One more dirty secret to add to the list.

The new customer sat down at a table. I adjusted my spaghetti straps and walked over to him. "Join you for a drink?" I asked mechanically.

"Sure," he said. "My name's James." James surprised me by ordering two plain sodas from the bar.

"So, what brings you to West Virginia?" I asked, not caring.

"I'm on assignment." I waited, but he didn't say any more. Instead he asked about me, what I wanted out of life. He talked as if I were a respectable person—which only made me more aware of my revealing costume. *Can't he see what I am?* I wondered.

"I'm due backstage," I said, getting up from my chair.

James stood up too and looked into my eyes. "Young lady," he said, "you were created for better things. God loves you. He can turn your life into something beautiful even now."

It seemed as if this man knew my secret, knew what had happened to me. But how could he? "I have to go . . ." I mumbled, completely shaken.

Backstage I thought about what James had said. Could things really be different for me? By the time I went back to James's table he was gone. The girls, the bouncers and bartenders, nobody remembered seeing the distinguished-looking customer.

After that encounter, I could no longer stomach my job. I quit the club and reenrolled at school. I'd have that better life, but this time it wouldn't be pretend. That meant I had to be honest—with myself and the people who cared about me. I would start with Danny. He deserved to know the truth.

Danny seemed skeptical as I settled into a chair across from him at his place. I took a deep breath. "There are things I should have told you before now . . ."

Somehow I got it all out.

Danny looked hurt. But I could see he was hurting for me. "Now I understand why you couldn't give our relationship a fair chance," he said gently.

Danny wanted to try again. We got back together. Or maybe I should say that for the first time we truly got together. I'd tried so hard to hide. But James showed me I didn't have to go to all that trouble. God knew my secrets and still loved me. Once I felt secure in his love, I accepted my husband's love too. And finally, after so long, I began to love myself again. I wonder if that wasn't the real assignment that brought James to West Virginia.

Heaven's Grandpa

KRISTINE E. BIXEL

Something brushed my hand and I stirred awake. There was my beloved grandpa Kegg beside me. He was holding my hand. "Honey, wake up," he said. I glanced around. I was in a hospital bed. What was happening? I felt panic until I looked at my grandfather's face. He always made me feel better, no matter what.

Family meant everything to me. I learned that growing up in Johnstown, Pennsylvania. I had love and support from my parents, my three brothers and especially my grandfather. I believed Grandpa Kegg knew everything, and he didn't mind a bit that I thought so. He lived right next door, so we kids were often at his house. Grandpa took a morning walk and sometimes we'd trail along. He had a favorite hat—a red plaid hunting cap—and he wore it year in, year out. "Guess what's in my pocket?" he'd ask. He might have had gum or a shiny nickel or a stone he'd rubbed till it shone. If one of us was worried about homework or trouble with a friend, he'd make silly noises to get us laughing. "*Quack, quack!*" he said once when I was feeling low. My mood brightened instantly. Whatever was wrong, Grandpa had that effect on me.

Still, I had trouble with my moods. My teenage years weren't easy. I was changing from a girl into a woman, and I didn't understand what I was feeling. Happy one minute, sad the next. Excited to be growing up and afraid of it at the same time. I was confused and somehow uncomfortable in my own skin. What was happening to me? Was I normal? In some ways my family all felt like strangers to me. I could talk with Grandpa Kegg about almost anything. But these feelings were something I couldn't express—to anyone. I kept everything bottled up. Kids at school made fun of me because I was withdrawn. I felt different, and I thought it was all my fault. I didn't know the word for it back then, but I was depressed most of the time.

"Something wrong with my little girl?" Grandpa Kegg asked one day. "No, I'm okay," I said and turned away. Grandpa put his hands on my shoulders and pivoted me back around. He could see that I was too old for silly duck quacks to cheer me up and that my troubles these days were more serious than a tiff with a friend. "Oh, honey," he said and hugged me tight. God and his angels could see me from heaven, but more than anyone on earth my grandpa understood me. I felt close to heaven in his arms.

As soon as I graduated from high school I decided to strike out on my own. "I think I'll go live in Florida," I said to my parents. "Just for a while." They thought maybe a change of scenery would do me some good.

I flew to Tampa, found a job and a room to rent. I liked the Gulf Coast and the warm, tropical air. One morning I walked along the bay, thinking of Grandpa in his red plaid cap. Life seemed very different here in Florida. *Maybe I can be different here too*, I thought. More like the little girl who used to laugh at Grandpa's silly duck quacks.

But I hadn't left my depression back home. Being on my own only made it worse. I looked for friends to fill my time between working. "Let's party!" a girl said to me in a bar one night. Turned out she was as troubled as I was, but she knew how to escape—alcohol and drugs. "Come on," she said. "Try it." I did. *What would Grandpa Kegg think of his little girl now?* I wondered. Before I knew it, I was "partying" every night. Instead of an escape from depression, my new lifestyle became another kind of trap.

By this time I'd become an expert at covering things up. I learned to hide my drinking just as I'd hidden my depression. No one knew the real me. I found a new job whenever I lost one and got through my twenties. But I couldn't hide from myself. I missed Grandpa. I missed my family. Finally I went back to Johnstown. But all the old insecurities waited for me there. Moving to Florida hadn't cured my depression, and it looked like moving back home wasn't going to cure my drug and alcohol addiction. Grandpa could see I was in more trouble than ever. I was grown up now, but the little girl in me still struggled for help.

One night I drank myself to the lowest point I'd ever known. I didn't want to go on with my life. I stumbled into the bathroom and opened the medicine chest. A full bottle of pills stared back at me. I filled a glass of water and swallowed every last one. I lay down on my bed. "Please, God, I can't fight anymore. Let me go to sleep and never wake up." I hoped the people I loved would forgive me.

Now, with Grandpa Kegg there beside me, I wondered how I'd wound up in this hospital bed. Grandpa was wearing his red plaid cap. *He's out for his morning walk,* I thought. *But why am I here?*

Grandpa looked very sad and kept patting my hand. "Honey, you have to wake up," he said. "Your life isn't over yet." Then I remembered what had happened. I was so embarrassed. Did Grandpa know what I'd done? I wanted to tell him everything. I knew he'd understand. I knew he'd still love me. And that—more than anything else—made me want to change my life. Looking into Grandpa's loving face, I knew I could do it. I had so much to say to him, but I was so tired. . . .

I must have drifted off to sleep. Mom was holding my hand when I woke up again. My whole family was there, everyone except my grandfather. "Where's Grandpa?" I mumbled.

"You've been asleep for three days," Mom said softly. "Your grandpa's been so afraid you'd never wake up, he hasn't left the house once."

I didn't argue. I knew in my heart that Grandpa had come to comfort me. As soon as I was discharged from the hospital I went to see him. He hugged me so tight he took my breath away. It was heaven to be in his arms again. "Your visit to the hospital changed me," I said. "I'll be the Kristine you've always known and loved. You'll see."

Grandpa looked at me with tears in his eyes. "But, Kristine, I didn't go to the hospital," he said. "I just couldn't."

"You must have gone during your daily walk. You wore your favorite cap."

"You know I couldn't have walked all the way to the hospital," Grandpa said. He was quiet, trying to make sense of what might have happened.

"I know it was you, Grandpa. You told me to wake up and I did."

Grandpa's eyes twinkled, as if he'd found an answer to our riddle. "Heaven wasn't ready for you," he said. "I suppose God sent an angel to tell you so."

Chills ran over me. My grandpa did know everything. And he knew that the heavenly angel who appeared to me in the hospital was meant to remind me of the earthly angel I'd loved and trusted all my life. And the angel was right. My life wasn't over. In fact, every day feels like a brand-new beginning.

12

COMING TO
CARRY US HOME

I looked over Jordan and what did I see,
Coming for to carry me home?
A band of angels coming after me,
Coming for to carry me home.
—Traditional Spiritual

Referring to a journey all of us will eventually make, this old song describes the final band in our procession of angels. Although we don't have reports of the ultimate "crossing over," occasionally someone is privileged to receive a special awareness of the attendants that accompany a loved one to his or her heavenly home. I trust you will keep reading to the very last story, "A Peek inside the Gate," in which a mother walks us through the process of letting go, realizing she can trust God's grace for herself and her son as he departs this world for "everlasting life beyond the gate."

In Momma's Room

MARY LOU SCHWADA

*B*oxes were stacked everywhere. The fireplace needed a cleaning. Padding hid the piano. Yet when I looked around our new house on moving day, I knew we'd found the perfect home. There was a big master bedroom for Terry and me, separate bedrooms for the girls, and best of all, a guest room for my parents. Now we wouldn't always have to travel to their house for visits. My whole life I'd felt safe and loved in Momma's house. More than anything I wanted to make her feel that way in mine.

She'd been diagnosed with Alzheimer's, and osteoporosis slowed her down. I wasn't sure how much longer she'd be able to travel, so I wanted to get right to work decorating. Singing to myself, I sliced open a box. *Just wait till I fix up the guest room,* I thought.

The bed was delivered, one with a nice firm mattress, just like Momma liked. The wallpaper and curtains suited Momma to a tee. The window looked out on our front yard. Everything was ready. But when I called Daddy to arrange a visit, he didn't think it was a good idea. "It's the five-hour drive," he said. "We just don't think we can make it right now."

Momma spent more and more time in the hospital. "The chances of her ever making the trip are slim," my sister Karen warned from back home.

That didn't stop me. I added a comfortable chair to the guest room, singing as I arranged it just so. *God, let Momma see this room I've prepared for her,* I asked. *Just once.*

The new chair gave me an idea. Momma was a big fan of the Marjorie Dean book series. I used to snuggle under my blankets as a child while Momma read volume after volume to me. She had been heartbroken when her set was destroyed in a flood. I'd replace them!

I scoured used bookstores and garage sales for early editions. Meantime, Karen investigated nursing homes for our momma. Daddy could no longer give her the round-the-clock care she needed.

"You don't have many more to go," Terry said as he watched me put my newly purchased *Marjorie Dean, High School Freshman* on the bookshelf. I nodded and ran my finger over the spines. Whenever we drove to Momma's house for a visit, I brought a volume with me.

By the time we'd really settled into our new house, the Marjorie Dean set was long since complete. Karen called one afternoon and told me she'd found a place for Momma. I drove up to help with the move. The nursing home was immaculate and the staff caring. Still, when I saw Momma's room, I couldn't help but think of the one I'd prepared for her.

A few weeks later I got a call: Momma had taken a turn for the worse. Terry and the girls helped me pack a bag. I left the next morning.

By early afternoon, Daddy, Karen and I were together at the nursing home. The doctors told us Momma probably did not have much time left.

Karen took Daddy home for a few hours' rest that evening. I settled in the chair beside Momma's bed. The oxygen tank hissed behind me. Momma took a labored breath. "I'm right here, Momma," I said.

How different this place was from the sunny room she had at my house. I imagined her sitting on the couch in the living room while the girls played piano. Terry would make a fire. Then before bed I would read to her from her brand-new Marjorie Dean collection.

God, she'll never know the love I had waiting for her in that room, will she? I thought wearily. I had to accept it.

I jerked my head up. "Is someone there?" I craned my neck to see the door. No one had come in. I squirmed in my seat. Something was definitely different. The air had gotten thicker. It was as if a throng of people had suddenly crowded into Momma's hospital room.

My mind's playing tricks. I pulled my chair a little closer to Momma's bed. She was sleeping peacefully, but I wanted to do something nice for her. "I'll sing you a song," I whispered. "I am standing on holy ground. . . ."

What was the next line? It was so hard to concentrate. I had the strange sensation I was singing before an audience. I scooted even closer to Momma, as if I needed to make room. For what? "I am standing on holy ground," I began again. I looked around. The words came.

"I am standing on holy ground," I sang. "And I know there are angels all around!"

The air seemed to burst with joy but not like any joy I had ever felt. This was joy I could almost touch. The joy of perfect love. The joy of heaven. Angels were all around me—I knew it! A host of angels had come for Momma. Was this what God had waiting for her? Momma's home on earth paled in comparison!

I leaned close to her. "I love you, Momma," I said. "And God loves you even more." Momma took two last sharp breaths and then exhaled. The presence I had felt all around me faded.

On my way to get a nurse, I remembered my prayer. I had asked God to give Momma a glimpse of my home. He had instead given me a glimpse of hers. God had prepared a place for Momma in heaven. A truly perfect place.

Hello from Heaven

ROBERTA LEY

When the phone rang at 11:30 PM, I always knew who was calling. "Hi, Berniece," I'd say. We had a routine, Berniece and I. She was my closest friend for thirty years, and we called each other every night. I couldn't remember exactly when we met, because I felt like I had always known her. So on a night in 1990 when the phone rang at 11:30, I reached for the receiver out of habit. But I hadn't spoken to Berniece for several days. She was in intensive care.

"Roberta!" said the sweet voice on the other end. There was no question. It was my friend. She sounded well and strong. I couldn't believe my ears.

Berniece and I lived nearby and we often got together, but the phone was our way of winding down after the three-to-eleven shift at our jobs. I was a proofreader for a publishing company, and Berniece worked at the Western Electric plant. Our houses were quiet when we got home, with our families fast asleep. I got in around 11:15, fixed a cup of tea and sat by the phone. Some nights I'd call and others I'd just wait for it to ring. "Thank God for telephones, right?" I said once. Berniece chuckled. Her job was assembling them down at the plant.

We had lots of laughs in those late-night calls. We prayed together too. Having Berniece on the phone was like having a direct line to heaven. She had a powerful faith, and she bolstered mine. Mostly we talked about our children. I had one son, but Berniece had a houseful—five children she'd embraced when she married their dad. I worried the marriage would never work out. "Love is the answer," Berniece said. "You'll see." For her, love was always the answer. Their home became one of the happiest I'd ever seen. She welcomed people at the door with a grin. "Just in time for cake," she'd say. Even with her job and the children, she made marvels in the kitchen. Many times I'd hear a knock, and it would be her daughter Tina: "Mom made too much chili. Here's some for you." Berniece knew I was crazy about her chili.

The main topic of conversation in our late-night calls continued to be our children as we struggled through their growing-up years. "Let's pray," she said one night. "God understands teenagers better than we do."

Eventually Berniece had to give up her job because her health was failing. She had diabetes and problems with her heart. She still called to chat at 11:30, but her voice was often weak.

When she was taken to the hospital in 1990, I wasn't able to see her. I was still working, and visiting hours were limited. But Tina kept me posted. "She promises to get well," Tina told me one day. "And she sends her love." Love was always the answer for Berniece.

Dear God, make her well again. Your love is the answer.

A few days later, Tina called, sounding worried. "Mom's getting worse," she said. That night I was thinking of Berniece and the phone rang at 11:30. Just like old times. "Berniece!" I said. "How are you?"

"You should see this!" she said. "An angel is smiling at me. An angel dressed in magenta and gold, his wings reaching the ceiling." I couldn't find words. My friend sounded so strong and excited. "Another angel is dressed in blue. They are so beautiful! I feel so good, Roberta. I'll be home in the morning." She hung up. *Angels with Berniece, how perfect.* And how like Berniece to want to share the vision with her best friend.

I slept soundly and woke with joy in my heart. There was a knock at my door. It was Tina. I pulled her inside. I blurted out about Berniece's call. "It couldn't be," Tina said quietly. "Mom died in her sleep last night. Around eleven thirty."

It couldn't be, but it was true. God had healed Berniece, and she was home, just as she'd said she would be. My phone had rung with a message from my friend, direct from heaven.

Gloria in the Hospital

ELLEN MILLER

Mattie was a tiny woman with enormous faith. She read her Bible daily and prayed for everyone who entered her room at the nursing home. Her mind was strong, but her body was racked with arthritis, osteoporosis and emphysema. Nevertheless, Mattie tried to live gracefully. As her nurse, I shared her struggles to walk, sleep, eat and bathe. She shared with me how much she missed her late husband and her second child, who had died as an infant.

I knew Mattie's children and grandchildren because of their regular visits. I thought I knew Mattie's whole family until she said, "Gloria came by again today." Her cousin Gloria's visits were becoming increasingly frequent according to Mattie, but somehow I had never once seen her.

One evening Mattie insisted, "She is standing right next to you." I saw no one, but a warm breeze swirled around me. I looked over at the window.

"Gloria is coming back tonight," Mattie said.

Later I was busy with other patients when an aide rushed to me. "It's Mattie."

I found her not breathing, not knowing Earth anymore. Then I felt another gentle breeze. The air rose and left as suddenly as it had come. Gloria had taken Mattie home. Was Gloria her cousin or her angel? Certainly she was someone from Mattie's heavenly family.

At the End of the Day

JEAN MILLER MEITZLER

No matter what kind of a day I had, it was a comfort to know it would end with Speeder and me sitting together in my easy chair. One winter night I petted her soft black fur. Her bottom lay curled in my lap, her graying head rested on my shoulder and she wrapped one black paw around my arm. Our peaceful nightly routine. I'd never forget the first time I saw her. My nephew showed up one day with two of his own dog's cocker-spaniel-mix puppies and told me to take my pick.

I watched the fat little balls of fur tumbling around on the floor and my heart melted, just as my nephew knew it would. "The price is right," he tempted me. "Free!"

My grandson Sam had been pestering me to get a puppy, so how could I resist? Naturally it was Sam who gave the puppy her name. "I guess we'll have to name her Blackie," he said. "Because she's all black."

"Nonsense. You can name her anything you want."

"Okay!" Sam said happily. "Then let's call her Speeder!" And so Speeder it was.

Sam was a young man now. Speeder was an old lady, like me. Neither one of us was too speedy anymore. Not like in the old days. My mother was still alive back then and living with Speeder and me. Each day when I left for work she waved to me from the front door, Speeder at her feet.

"Be a good girl, Speeder," I said one morning, leaning down to scratch her ears. "Keep Mother company while I'm gone."

I turned to go. Halfway down the front walk I heard, "Speeder! Come back!" I stopped short as a black blur ran past me and raced down the block. "I don't know how she slipped out!" Mother said.

I ran after her. She stopped and sat down to wait for me. Just as I reached her she ran off again—this time toward the house! Back and forth four times before I finally caught the rascal. "You made sure I got my workout this morning, didn't you?" I said.

Speeder barked happily.

My "morning workout" became a habit. In broiling Texas heat, under pouring rain and over sidewalks slick with ice, you could find me in my business suit, chasing Speeder. "Those were the days, weren't they, old girl?"

Speeder looked up at me, her eyes searching mine for reassurance. Once those eyes were deep brown. Now they were cloudy with cataracts. I'd had mine removed with surgery.

"What's the matter? Is your arthritis bothering you?" My own arthritis was known to flare up when I'd been sitting for a while.

I helped her into her dog bed on the floor. Speeder had had a series of strokes that sometimes made it hard for her to balance, but she settled herself happily in her bed and hung her head off the side, her favorite position—besides my lap.

I went to my own bed. *How many more nights will she be with me?* I wondered.

My veterinarian had a poem in his office that described a beautiful rainbow bridge connecting heaven and earth. All animals crossed over the bridge when they died. On the other side old dogs became young again and romped and played forever in the endless green fields, waiting for the people they loved.

"Lord," I said when I was tucked under my covers, "when it's her time, please let Speeder die in peace. Let her run happily over that rainbow bridge."

A few weeks later I took Speeder to the animal hospital for a bath. When I returned to pick her up, the attendant had some bad news. "Speeder seems weak," she said. "She may have had another stroke."

She carried Speeder to my car, wrapped in a blanket. Her breathing was shallow and her eyes looked glazed. I carried Speeder into the house, right to our easy chair. I held her on my lap and stroked her head. "We're home, Speeder," I said softly. "Don't worry. I won't leave you."

Speeder lifted her head to my shoulder and wrapped her paw around my arm. We stayed right there until we both fell asleep. Sometime after midnight Speeder started to cry. I could see she was in pain. Her breathing became harsh and shallow.

"Lord," I said, "please send me an angel to help Speeder through this. If it is her time, let these moments be happy and peaceful. Please send an angel into our home!"

The words were barely out of my mouth when I felt a real change in the room. Someone—something?—had entered. I could feel it. Speeder and I were no longer alone. I looked around, but there was no one there, no one I could see. But what was that? In a chair against the far wall. Out of the corner of my eye I saw a black dog with deep brown eyes, just like Speeder. When I looked at the chair directly it was empty, but as soon as I turned my head the slightest bit, I could spot the dog out of the corner of my eye.

"Speeder," I whispered, "I think the Lord sent you an angel—a dog to comfort you."

Speeder whined and struggled in my lap, signaling that she needed to go outside. I carried her into the backyard. The angel dog came with us. It floated beside me, about waist high to the left and just behind me, barely visible if I sneaked a peek.

I gently put Speeder on the grass, and the angel dog disappeared. When I carried Speeder back inside I couldn't see our comforting friend, but I could still feel its presence, strong as ever.

Speeder's breathing grew calm. She looked tired but not uncomfortable. I laid her in her dog bed right beside my chair, her head hanging off the side the way she liked. Speeder reached out one small paw to touch my chair, sleeping as peacefully as she had when she was only a puppy. I breathed easily too. Speeder was not in pain, and she wasn't alone. She had me beside her, an angel to guide her and the good Lord waiting to welcome her to heaven.

At about eight o'clock in the morning, Speeder's breathing slowed and stopped. At the same moment the presence disappeared. I knew as sure as I knew anything that Speeder's angel had escorted her over the rainbow bridge. Good old Speeder will be there waiting when my own angel leads me over, at the peaceful end of day.

A Peek inside the Gate

GWEN BRADFORD SPELL

My son Matt was diagnosed with leukemia at the end of April. He was sixteen years old. We made the trip from our home in Louisiana and checked him into St. Jude Hospital in Memphis, Tennessee, for chemotherapy. Prayer sustained Matt—and our entire family—through those brutal months. No matter what happened, Matt kept an unshakable faith that God would heal him. After several chemo treatments and a stem-cell transplant from his father, the leukemia seemed to go into remission. Matt stayed at St. Jude so that his health could be monitored, but I slowly got used to the idea that God had performed a miracle. He had saved my son.

If only. In December Matt relapsed. I knew that his chances of recovering again were slim at best. Matt knew it too. He never talked about it, though. Instead, we all tried our best to be hopeful and upbeat.

"I have one hundred percent faith," Matt said.

But Matt didn't respond to chemo this time. The medication again made him sick and weak. One night, I lay beside Matt in the hospital bed, rubbing his thin back, trying to help him sleep. He was discouraged. So was I. *Matt needs me to be strong,* I told myself.

His breathing grew more regular, and I knew he was asleep. I switched off the light and stared up at the dark ceiling. *Lord, what's going to happen to my son?* Tears came to my eyes, and I pushed my face into the pillow. Lying there in that hospital bed, I thought of the day Matt was born, November 3—my twenty-first birthday. God wouldn't take my birthday baby away from me, would he?

I squeezed my eyes shut, pushing away that possibility. Suddenly I wasn't in the hospital anymore. I was standing in front of a beautiful gate. On the other side I saw a group of ladies. Among them were Matt's great-grandmothers, both deceased.

"Is Matthew coming?" one of the ladies asked.

"No, not today," another said. "Maybe soon."

I opened my mouth to tell them that Matt wasn't coming at all, that he was going to get better, but the scene dissolved. I was back in the hospital again.

I got up carefully, so as not to wake Matt, and spread out my blanket and pillow on the sofa. My heart was pounding. Images from the vision swirled in my mind. What did it mean? Why had I seen this glimpse of heaven? Was God trying to tell me something? About Matthew?

No. There's still time for a miracle. There has to be.

In the next few weeks, hope became harder to hold onto. Alternative chemo treatments weren't working. The doctors couldn't control Matt's white blood cell count. Matt fought hard, but the leukemia had returned with a vengeance.

Matt put on a brave face.

"How's my favorite patient?" the nurse would ask each day.

"I feel just fine," Matt invariably replied, even on the worst days. Sometimes I even believed him. My husband, Anthony, arranged to stay with us full time. Tyler, Matt's younger brother, switched to a school in Memphis so that he could be there too. Friends and family came and went.

I spent most days sitting by Matt's bed, crocheting blankets and doing cross-stitch. When Matt was too weak to do anything else, he would hold the yarn for me and make sure it didn't get tangled.

"When I get out of here, Mom," he told me, "we're gonna sit on the couch at home and drink a pitcher of lemonade."

I didn't tell Matt about the vision I'd had. I didn't tell anyone. Sometimes, when I shut my eyes, the image of the gate appeared again. I tried to ignore it. *Maybe it doesn't mean what I think it does,* I told myself. *Maybe it's just my imagination.* But there was only so long I could deny it.

One night in January I kissed Matt good-night and lay down on the couch. The room fell away. I was standing in front of the gate. Matt's two great-grandmothers stood just inside. Their eyes twinkled. They seemed excited. They were waiting for someone.

I turned, and in the distance I saw a figure approaching. It was Matt. He looked thin and tired. His face was gaunt. His steps were slow. Instantly I knew what this meant. I was the only person standing between Matt and the gate, between my son and death. *No, Lord. I can't let him pass through.* I curled up at the foot of the gate and closed my eyes. A gentle voice said, "It's okay, Gwen. You can sleep here. It's not time yet."

On February 14, we learned that Matt had pneumonia brought on by his weakened immune system. One of his lungs had collapsed. His doctors had tried every kind of treatment, but leukemia had consumed my son's body. "I'm sorry," the head doctor finally told us, "there's nothing more we can do. We can care for him here or you can take him home. Either way, he has a few days at most."

Matt and I made the long trip back to Louisiana in an ambulance. Anthony, Tyler, friends and family followed by car in one big caravan. I sat beside Matt the whole way, holding his hand. Bad as things were, I grasped at any shred of hope. Part of me wanted to believe that when we got home, Matt would put on his sneakers and run out into the yard to play football with Tyler.

We pulled up in our driveway. It was good to be home. *Lord, if you're planning a miracle, today's the day.*

We put Matt in a bed in the living room. On February 19, his breathing became slow and painful. Each breath seemed like it could be his last. I couldn't stand to see my son suffer. I thought about the people behind the gate, how happy and peaceful they seemed. Would he be better off there? I tried to think of Matt and not myself, but I couldn't imagine living in a world without him. *God, he can't die. Not my baby.*

Night fell. Still Matt hung on. His breathing became labored until finally it stopped.

I leaned over his bed, holding his hand and counted the seconds, *One . . . two . . . three. No, this couldn't be.* "Matt!"

I looked up at the dark window over his bed. Two figures in long white robes were there, backs to me, hands crossed to form a seat. Between them, facing me, sat Matt. He was thin and sickly like the boy in the bed, but he wore a pristine white robe. I could see he was worried about me. *Mom, this is it,* he seemed to say. *Can I go?*

I froze. The breath caught in my throat. Matt was waiting for my answer. His eyes pleaded for me to tell him it was okay. I put my lips down close to his ear on the pillow. "Go home, Matt," I whispered. "Go on home."

Matt let out a long, gentle sigh—a last breath full of relief and peace. I looked toward the window and watched the angels carry my birthday baby away, out into the darkness, toward a single, bright pinpoint of light. Of hope. Of health and happiness and everlasting life beyond the gate.

About the Editor

Evelyn Bence is the editor of *Comfort from Beyond, A Closer Walk with Jesus* and *We Hear the Christmas Angels*, the author of *Spiritual Moments with the Great Hymns, Prayers for Girlfriends and Sisters and Me*, and titles in the Women of Faith series, and a contributor to *Daily Guideposts*. Her novel *Mary's Journal* won a *Christianity Today* critics' award. Evelyn lives in Arlington, Virginia.

A Note from the Editors

Guideposts, a nonprofit organization, touches millions of lives every day through products and services that inspire, encourage and uplift. Our magazines, books, prayer network and outreach programs help people connect their faith-filled values to their daily lives. To learn more, visit www.guideposts.com or www.guidepostsfoundation.org.